The Wonder of Trees

The Wonder of Trees

Nature Activities for Children

Andrea Frommherz and Edith Biedermann

Floris Books

Translated by Bernadette Duncan

First published in German under the title
Kinderwerkstatt Bäume by AT Verlag 2003
This English edition published in 2012

© 2003 AT Verlag, Aurau and Munich
Photographs by Andrea Frommherz, Patrick Weyeneth,
Cuno Frommherz and Tobias Hauser
Illustrations by Edith Biedermann

British Library CIP Data available
ISBN 978-086315-866-7
Printed in China

Contents

Introduction

TREE MEMORIES

The magic of trees, their mystical qualities, secrets and wisdom have long since fascinated people. Encounters with trees always leave traces. Trees are living beings, their gestures and shapes, their manifold expressions, sturdiness and lightness, their connection to the depths of the earth and to the sky above fill me with enthusiasm. Sometimes I make up stories about a tree, let myself be taken on a journey back to its youth or simply let myself be enchanted.

Trees are all around us – beside our houses, at the side of the road, in the park, in the meadow, on the playground, in the woods and in the garden. Trees differ in the manner in which their branches and twigs grow and in the way their buds, leaves, needles, blossoms and fruit are formed. By always remaining in the same place, trees become something familiar to us in an ever-changing world. A tree – with its greening in spring and its wilting in autumn – symbolises life and death. During the course of the seasons a tree's vitality is renewed. The cycle of flowering, growing, propagation and rest may be compared to the life of a human being. Trees are living beings which existed before our birth and will outlive us. The trees that we know today will contribute to the lives of our grandchildren and great-grandchildren.

I get attracted to certain trees at various times in my life. They mirror my particular situation, my hopes and dreams. When I was a child, a hazel bush was a close confidant. As young adults, we had a lovely time chatting, singing and making music under the lime tree on the hill above the village; here, too, first love was stirring. While I was studying, the birches outside my window lightened the many hours spent poring over my books. Later I made friends under the chestnut trees of a cosy pub. My first conscious encounter with a huge ash tree growing behind a friend's house made a lasting impression on me; this tree even appeared to me in dreams a few times. And an elderflower tree has just crept into my present garden – I can't wait for the first buds to grow and for summertime, when we will be able to lie in the shade of the overhanging branches.

Where is that tree which is engrained in your memory and feelings, and which still accompanies you strongly today?

THE TREE 'SHOPPING CENTRE'

Imagine yourself many decades back: trees were used as a kind of shopping centre for all of life's necessities. They have a food and a non-food section, a health and a service sector. You can get anything. Fruit, leaves, sap and bark all serve as food or medicines. Wood is a source of energy for cooking and warmth. Leaves are used as animal feed and fertilizer, ashes as washing suds. People use wood to make their homes, tools and toys. They use it to build vehicles, ships, art objects

and musical instruments. Trees mark borders, they act as road signs and offer protection against the wind. And last but not least, they form part of our recreational spaces, they are the habitat of countless animals and also an important supplier of oxygen.

RITUAL IMPORTANCE

For many people trees represent the basic laws of life, they symbolise wisdom and strength. They are often believed to be sanctuaries, the dwelling places of deities.

A tree is an extraordinarily diverse symbol: it stands for protection, shade, shelter, the elixir of life, being grounded, old age or personality. The greening of trees marks the beginning of spring, and trees play an important part in harvest festivals too. They help to preserve fertility and keep away disasters, diseases and lightning. Numerous customs are associated with trees and many fairy stories, songs and poems celebrate their qualities.

Nowadays, we are no longer aware of a tree as an individual with all its manifold characteristics. Over the past decades we've viewed trees primarily for their biological importance, and as useful suppliers of wood and energy. So let us rediscover trees again in all their facets!

Below, the cotyledons; above, the first tender leaves of a young beech.

THE THIRTEEN TREES

In this book we meet thirteen common trees and shrubs, woven into the cycle of the year, with activities for each season. For each tree, we highlight one aspect of its nature, which corresponds to a key skill that we use in everyday life.

Cultures descended from the Germanic people, and the cultural history of Europe in general, are closely connected with trees, forests and all kinds of mysterious beings that dwell in the vicinity of trees. That's the reason why airy elves and earthy gnomes accompany us throughout the book.

The selection of games, recipes, songs and stories will encourage children, young people and adults to develop a creative approach to trees while using all their senses, exploring the diverse relationship between trees and humans. Different parts of trees are the ingredients for a number of recipes for medicinal and culinary use. Following simple instructions, we can glimpse how trees play a significant role in our nutrition and health. Since rituals are of great importance in human lives, they form an integral part of this book. Of course, they have changed and evolved over the centuries and have been adapted to new needs.

Plant identification games are deliberately not included. There is an ample range of good quality publications and books on these kinds of games. Yet this book is full of practical ideas for projects, games and crafts to experience the qualities of the individual tree types. The activities can easily be adjusted according to the age and knowledge of the children or group you are working with.

THE MESSAGE OF TREES

Trees accompany us through life. They are our friends and teachers. If we allow ourselves to be touched by the wisdom and vitality of a tree and if we listen to it, we will be able to unlock and understand its secret messages. It is communicating with us through its shape and its qualities, its healing properties, its place in folklore, its physical location. Every tree has a message that can support human beings and help find answers to life's questions.

We are constantly faced with new demands and challenges both in our personal and professional lives. Through rapid changes at school, in the workplace and in our environment, we are constantly having to learn new skills. Therefore today, more than ever before, people need to be equipped with the tools to deal with change. In this book, we'll refer to these skills as 'key skills'. They don't only enable us to respond to a particular situation, but are useful for life in general.

In the long run, a skilled person without social abilities is not easy to work with; it's difficult to live with a partner who cannot reflect on life; a pupil who does not believe in herself will not achieve good results. It's these same skills that enable people to adopt a sustainable approach to nature. If we listen to the messages of trees, we'll be able to deepen our relationship with the earth, with ourselves and with other people.

Because there are so many archetypal symbols in nature, we wanted to work with nature on a personal level too. So for each of the thirteen trees, we worked out a particular message, a particular section in the field of key skills.

THE WONDER OF TREES

The purpose of focusing on trees is not just to practise environmentally sound behaviour. The aim is rather to nourish and deepen our own souls, to develop an appreciation for ourselves, for others and for nature. This will not come about through rules and regulations or a moralising attitude but through actually feeling, experiencing, thinking and doing.

I hope this book will awaken people's desire to rediscover the wonder of trees, to understand their messages and to use the knowledge thus gained in daily life.

Pieces of wood marked with symbols encourage conversation.

Basic recipes for preparing tree products

With the help of various liquids we can obtain the active ingredients of plants. In herbalism this is called a plant extract. Plant extracts serve as a basis for various medicines.

Water-based extracts: pour water over the plant parts or soak them in water. Water-based extracts are used for tea, baths, face tonics, ointments and poultices.

Oil-based extracts: steep the plant parts in plant oil so they are completely covered. Uses for oil-based extracts include massage oil and ointments.

Vinegar-based extracts: steep the plant parts in vinegar. This fluid is then processed to prepare various herbal remedies.

Alcohol-based extracts: steep the plant parts in alcohol. Alcohol-based plant extracts are called tinctures and may be added to shaving tonics or lotions.

TEA

For preparing tea, various parts of the tree can be used: blossoms (e.g. lime flowers), leaves (e.g. birch leaves), fruit (e.g. rose hips) or bark (e.g. willow bark).

Take one teaspoon of dried or two teaspoons of fresh plant substances per cup. An infusion is the most common method of making tea. Put the herbs (mostly flowers or leaves) into a cup or jug and add boiling water. Let the mixture steep for 5–10 minutes. If the plants used contain essential oils, cover the container. The aromatic oils will condense on the underneath side of the lid and drip back into the tea. After straining, the tea is ready to drink; sweeten with honey according to taste.

For woody plant parts such as bark and roots, whose active ingredients are only extracted into the water after a longer period of cooking, a decoction is a more suitable way of making tea. Put the chopped plant parts into cold water, bring to the boil and simmer for 15–30 minutes; strain the tea whilst still hot.

Examples
Birch-leaf tea, lime-flower tea, rose-hip tea, rose-petal tea, apple-peel tea, elderflower tea, spruce-needle tea, walnut-leaf tea.

EXTRACTS MADE WITH OIL, VINEGAR OR ALCOHOL

5 parts (500 ml, 1/2 quart) oil, vinegar or alcohol
1 part (1 handful of fresh or 1/2 handful of dried)
    plant parts

Let the mixture dry in the sun in a closed container for 2–3 weeks. With the sunlight other subtle forces are carried into the fluid. In winter you can let the plant extract steep in a warm place in the house. Shake the contents from time to time.

Strain the plant extract and keep in glass jars or bottles.

Examples
Oil extracts: birch oil, spruce oil, rose oil,
    walnut oil
Vinegar extracts: birch vinegar, rose vinegar
Alcohol extracts (tinctures): birch tincture

SYRUP

5 handfuls fresh plant parts
1 litre (1 quart) water
1 kg (2 1/4 lb) sugar

Put the plant parts into the water and bring to the boil. Let it cool, strain and add the sugar. Boil it down to a syrupy consistency and store in a bottle.

Examples
Spruce syrup, apple syrup, elderflower syrup, nutshell syrup.

Opposite: Trees give energy and peace

Tree products can be pretty to look at and delicious to eat

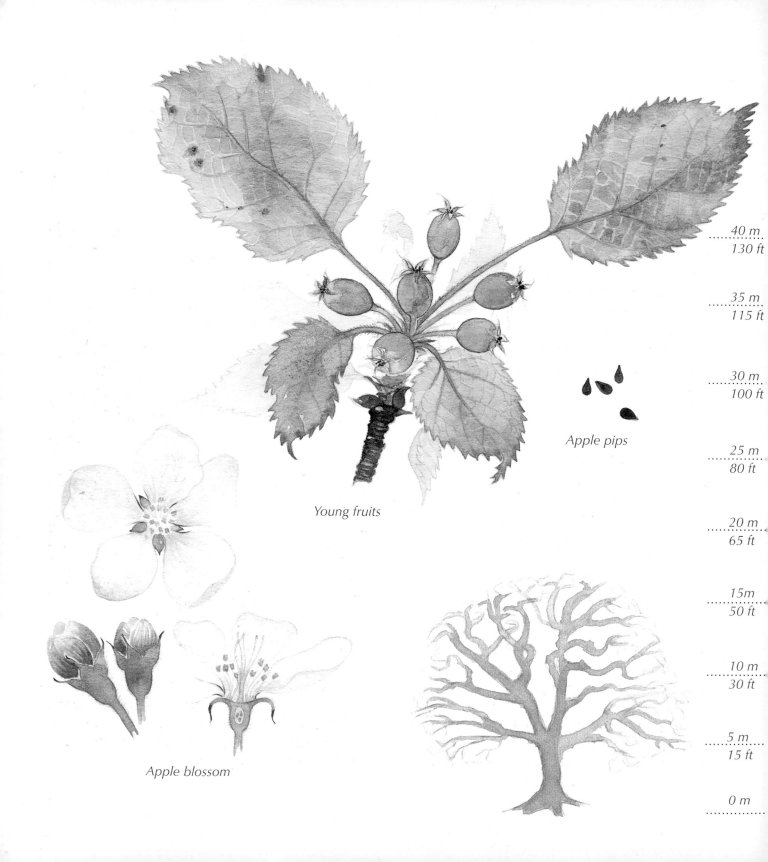

Young fruits

Apple pips

Apple blossom

40 m
130 ft

35 m
115 ft

30 m
100 ft

25 m
80 ft

20 m
65 ft

15m
50 ft

10 m
30 ft

5 m
15 ft

0 m

1. Apple – Tree of Self-knowledge

HABITAT AND CHARACTERISTICS

The apple tree probably originated in central and western India, although we can't ascertain its origin for certain. We believe that people have tried to cultivate the apple tree from very early on. It was the Romans who introduced the first grafted apple trees to Europe. Then only a few different kinds existed. Nowadays a wide range of cultivated apple tree varieties exist throughout the world.

The crab apple is the common ancestor of all apple tree varieties. It likes to grow in light-filled woodlands, at the edge of woods or in hedges. Unlike cultivated apple trees, the crab apple has thorns and its fruit tend to stay small. These ancient apples are barely edible and very sour when uncooked. However, when added to apple recipes, crab apples can intensify the flavour. Deer love the fruit of the crab-apple tree.

ALL SORTS OF USES

Besides the fruit, which has always been an important part of people's diet, the wood of the apple tree can be used for making gifts and tools. It's also excellent for carving.

The apple has some surprises in store when it comes to our physical well-being. An apple facemask has anti-ageing properties – it cleanses the skin and makes it more elastic: cook an apple in milk until soft, mash it with a fork to form a paste and apply to the face. An oil extract made with apple blossoms is a good ingredient for bath oil. Thinned down apple-blossom tincture is a good facial cleansing tonic.

Spring

KEY SKILL: SELF-KNOWLEDGE AND SELF-ACCEPTANCE

Although most of the apple trees known to us tend to be cultivated varieties, they have retained many of the original characteristics of traditional apple trees. If a cultivated apple tree is left to grow naturally, it will soon resemble its ancestor. Just as every tree is an individual being, each person is unique. Everyone has his or her own character, which in the course of life is subjected to a wide range of influences. It's important to know our own character and tendencies and to accept them, in order to develop a healthy self-confidence. This includes understanding both our strengths and our weaknesses. We have to learn to have a realistic picture of ourselves and to develop according to our inclinations and abilities. If you over- or underestimate yourself, you won't be able to live in peace with your surroundings. To come to know yourself is a lifelong process, and we all need support along the way.

Observing an apple tree from spring to autumn

It is fascinating to watch the development of an apple tree from spring to autumn. In spring its blossoms unfold even before the leaves appear. In the course of a few months the tiny hard fruits grow into delicious autumn apples.

During the various seasons we can sit down near the tree and observe it. What is its shape? What does its bark look like? Where does it stand? We can try to describe in a few words what is special about this tree, and then see what we can learn from the tree.

What do blossoms symbolise in human life? What do scars mean in human life? What does fruit mean in human life?

Opposite: Tree pantomime, enacting tree characteristics

Listening to your tree

16

Paintings of trees can convey our personalities

Tree pantomime

Discuss the characteristics of various trees and agree on how you can characterise and 'act' these trees. When somebody calls out the name of a tree, the actors try to portray this tree as quickly as possible. If somebody acts out a trait that doesn't belong to this tree, a forfeit has to be given.

Painting our tree-selves

Trees can represent the developmental processes of human beings in a symbolic way, and can help us to explore various aspects of ourselves. In doing so trees – beyond their concrete outer appearance – can symbolise the self and our own frame of mind.

We can imagine what we would look like as a tree. Children should decide what kind of tree they would like to be. How big should it be? Which particular shape? Which colours should it have? Should it bear blossoms or fruit? Should it be an old or a young tree? Do its gesture, its size, its annual rings, its contortions speak of a good life or of much suffering? A certain season and certain surroundings may belong to this tree. It may also be a fantasy tree.

We can then paint our trees and share them with the group. Since the tree is a picture of our own personality, we can use this exercise to get to know each other better within the group.

Variation 1. Lay the tree pictures in a circle, and ask everyone to explain their tree from the perspective of the tree itself: 'I am a young apple tree. This year I bear fruit for the first time. The birds love to sing in my branches' etc. The others can ask questions (but it's important not to interpret the paintings without being asked).

Variation 2. Collect the tree paintings, mix them up and lay them in the middle of the group. The group then guesses who painted each picture.

Family trees

Family histories, which may even span a few centuries, are often depicted in the shape of a tree. Looking into our family history helps us to understand our own past and our own roots. Family trees often trace the line of the male members of the family. It can be equally interesting to create a family tree which shows the line of our female ancestors.

Making tree friends

People often feel attracted to certain trees. Ask your group to look for a tree nearby which they like. This becomes 'their' tree. First everyone should spend some time just quietly being with a chosen tree. Then we can look at it more closely and investigate it. We can feel the bark and the leaves. We can listen to any sounds coming from the tree, and see if the tree is speaking to us. We may hug our tree and stay like that for a moment. The idea is to concentrate fully on the tree for a few minutes and to 'grow together' with it. The tree can become a good friend.

Then something unexpected happened, actually something very beautiful: after a while I noticed only the usual sounds in the wood. Apart from that it was and remained absolutely still.

When I called the children after 45 minutes all of them returned unusually calm and quiet. They seemed visibly moved, fulfilled, touched by something indescribable. Over the days that followed they continued to visit 'their' trees. At the end of the week a girl wrote in her daily report, 'Now my tree is my friend. I can tell it everything, it listens to me and doesn't pass on to anyone else what I say.'

(Fritz Graber, teacher, Germany)

Summer

HOME REMEDIES

Even Stone-Age man knew the apple tree. Its fruit has always been an important part of our daily diet. Apples are tasty and healthy and may be used both as food and medicine. Apples have many precious components: vitamins, minerals and trace elements. There are many uses for apples in traditional medicine, but only a few of them are described here.

Apples strengthen the body's defences. Depending on how they are prepared, the digestive properties of apples vary. Apples are calming, appetising and diuretic; they can help lower fevers and support the treatment of rheumatoid diseases. They are also suitable for use in weight-loss diets.

Regularly eating apples is good for your health. Everyone knows the saying, 'An apple a day keeps the doctor away.' Growing children in particular benefit from apples. Since raw apples are difficult to digest, they should not be eaten during illness or before going to bed.

Opposite: No apple tastes better

Apples for flu, fever or diarrhoea

Steamed or stewed apples: stew apples in a little water until soft. Stewed apples are a healthy and light dish to eat when you have gastric flu and fevers.

Grated apples: leave a grated apple until it turns brown. Eat a spoonful at a time, chewing slowly and thoroughly. This is effective against diarrhoea.

Apple (peel) tea

Tea prepared from the peel and pulp of apples is tasty, relaxing, refreshing and strengthening. Sweetened with honey, apple tea in particular calms the nerves. It also has a stimulating effect on the kidneys and bladder and is recommended for fevers and infections.

Apple peel may be used fresh or dried. Dry the bits of peel in the sun or in the oven at a low temperature (50°C, 122°F). For making tea, pour 1 cup of boiling water over 2 teaspoons of fresh or dried apple peel and let the mixture steep for a few minutes. This tea can also be combined with rose-hip or pear peel.

Or peel 3–4 apples and chop into small bits. Bring them to the boil in 1/2 litre (1/2 quart) of water and let it steep for 30 minutes.

Drying apple rings

Apple syrup

Bring equal parts of chopped apples and water to the boil, then strain. Add the same weight in sugar and boil down to a syrupy consistency. This is especially suitable for children suffering from a cough, sore throat or fever.

Further recommendations

Apple-onion paste relieves a cough.

Apple wine can be used to treat stress and exhaustion.

Apply an apple poultice (grated apple paste in a cloth) to bruises.

For a sore throat, eat baked apples.

Autumn

HARVEST FESTIVAL

In autumn, when fruit, nuts and vegetables are harvested, people have always celebrated harvest festivals, with food, dancing, merriment and tables decorated with harvest offerings. In the olden days this was a way of thanking the gods, so they would provide a rich harvest the following year, as food gathered from fields, woods and meadows was of vital importance. Even today some farmers keep to the old custom of leaving the last apple on the tree. In doing so they express their gratitude to the tree and ask for an ample harvest in the year to come.

Apples are versatile ingredients in food. They can be eaten raw, baked, stewed, grated or fried. You can prepare desserts such as stewed apples, apple fool, apple jelly, apple cake, apple strudel, apple bake, apple sauce, various beverages and even apple soup. Organic apples are healthiest and in a cool cellar they keep very well.

APPLE RECIPES FROM PICNIC TO PUDDING

Apple rings
Slice the apples thinly and cut out the core of each slice. Thread the apple rings onto a piece of string and let them air-dry for a few days. Apple rings are tasty snacks to take on outings.

Apple soup
Cook finely sliced apples together with some cinnamon and lemon rind in water until soft. Strain the spices and thicken with some flour. Sweeten with sugar according to taste.

Apple salad
Grate apples and carrots (celeriac and beetroot may also be used) and add salad dressing.

Baked apples
Filling for 4 apples:
1 1/2 tablespoons quark
1 egg yolk
a little cinnamon
1 tablespoon honey
2 teaspoons chopped almonds or hazelnuts
   (optional: a few raisins)
1 tablespoon lemon juice

Spoon the mixture into the cored apples. Place on a greased tray and bake in the oven at a medium heat for 20–30 minutes.

Apples can also be baked on a stick over the fire. Before eating, sprinkle with cinnamon and sugar.

Listening to a tree story

Apple omelettes

Fry thinly sliced apples in butter. Dust with a bit of sugar and add some cream. Use this mixture as a filling for omelettes.

Apple trifle

In a bowl, arrange layers of sponge fingers, custard and cooked apple slices. Refrigerate until cool.

Apple milk

2–3 sour apples
1/2 litre (1/2 quart) water
1/2 litre (1/2 quart) milk

Grate the apples, add to the water/milk mixture and bring to the boil. Strain and serve cold. A refreshing and healthy snack-time drink.

Apple jam

See instructions for elderberry jam, p.105.

Winter

THE SYMBOLIC APPLE

The apple tree and its fruit have a prominent place in the folklore of many cultures. The tree symbolises nature with her nurturing qualities. It is a tree of life and stands for both life and death. The fruit and wood of the apple tree are used in magic rites, which were performed, for example, to win over a chosen person. The apple was also used as an oracle of love. It represents love, fertility, knowledge and sin but also youth and immortality. Thanks to its enticing colour and sweetness it often symbolises sensual charm. Both the apple and the apple tree play important parts in countless stories, fairy tales and legends. The apple is mentioned in many religious books, which tell of wonderful trees bearing golden apples and supposedly giving eternal life; whoever eats one of the magic apples remains forever young. In some stories the apple also symbolises the trials we face during life's journey; our hero's travels often lead him to the tree of life guarded by dangerous animals. Goddesses often use the apple to show the path to perfection.

Jesus Christ the Apple Tree

The tree of life my soul hath seen,
Laden with fruit and always green:
The trees of nature fruitless be
Compared with Christ the apple tree.

His beauty doth all things excel:
By faith I know, but ne'er can tell
The glory which I now can see
In Jesus Christ the apple tree.

For happiness I long have sought,
And pleasure dearly I have bought:
I missed of all; but now I see
'Tis found in Christ the apple tree.

I'm weary with my former toil,
Here I will sit and rest awhile:
Under the shadow I will be,
Of Jesus Christ the apple tree.

This fruit doth make my soul to thrive,
It keeps my dying faith alive;
Which makes my soul in haste to be
With Jesus Christ the apple tree.

(Anonymous hymn)

Apple-themed fairy tales by the Brothers Grimm

Presently the King's daughter herself came down into the garden, and was amazed to see that the young man had done the task she had given him. But she could not yet conquer her proud heart, and said, 'Although he has performed both the tasks, he shall not be my husband until he has brought me an apple from the Tree of Life.'

The youth did not know where the Tree of Life stood, but he set out, and would have gone on forever, as long as his legs would carry him, though he had no hope of finding it. After he had wandered through three kingdoms, he came one evening to a wood and lay down under a tree to sleep. But he heard a rustling in the branches, and a golden apple fell into his hand...

(Brothers Grimm, *The White Snake*)

In the fairy tales of the Brothers Grimm, the apple and the apple tree are frequent symbols.

The White Snake: the princess demands an apple from the tree of life from her suitor. Once this condition is fulfilled she eventually gives him her heart.

One-Eye, Two-Eyes and Three-Eyes: a tree with golden leaves and fruit is growing in front of the house. Only Two-Eyes is able to pick the apples.

Snow White: the stepmother poisons Snow White with an apple.

Iron Hans: the disguised gardener's boy and knight catches the golden apple at every feast and escapes undiscovered.

Mother Holly: only the hard-working girl shakes the apple tree. The lazy one gets punished and covered with tar.

The King's Son Who Feared Nothing: before the wedding can take place, the giant first has to get an apple from the tree of life for his bride-to-be.

The Devil With The Three Golden Hairs: a riddle involving a tree with golden apples has to be solved.

The Golden Bird: golden apples are stolen from the tree in the king's garden.

2. Birch – Tree of Flexibility

HABITAT AND CHARACTERISTICS

The birch with its shimmering white bark and gently stirring twigs is a graceful, delicate tree. It's only over time that black marks appear in the bark. Then it seems as if the birch is looking with furrowed bark eyebrows into the world.

The birch is one of our oldest trees. Soon after the last Ice Age subsided it started to populate the still barren wetlands. As a pioneer species it is still planted today in wet or clear-felled areas and wastelands in order to stabilise slopes and embankments and to help drain the land. Birch grows in the northern hemisphere amongst other trees in woods, at the side of the road, in meadows, on riverbanks or in gardens. With its air-cushioned bark it can even stand cold northerly climates. In the Alps it grows up to an altitude of 2,000 metres (1 1/4 miles). The birch is a very thirsty tree and on warm summer days it may absorb up to 70 litres (70 quarts) of water.

ALL SORTS OF USES

In olden times all parts of the birch – leaves, roots, wood and buds – were made use of. Roofs were covered with the waterproof and insulating bark. The North American native people used it to build their canoes. The bark of a young birch is soft and subtle, and it was used to make shoes or cloaks. Bast fibres made from the inner bark served as raw material for dresses. And in times of need this yellowish inner bark was scraped off, chopped up, dried and ground to make 'birch flour' for bread. The birch's bark and wood contain pitch, which was used to seal boats and containers and to treat leather. Hunters used to strengthen their arrowheads with birch pitch. The wood even burns when it's fresh and damp because of its pitch content, which is why birch shavings make good kindling. A birch-wood fire burns with very bright flames.

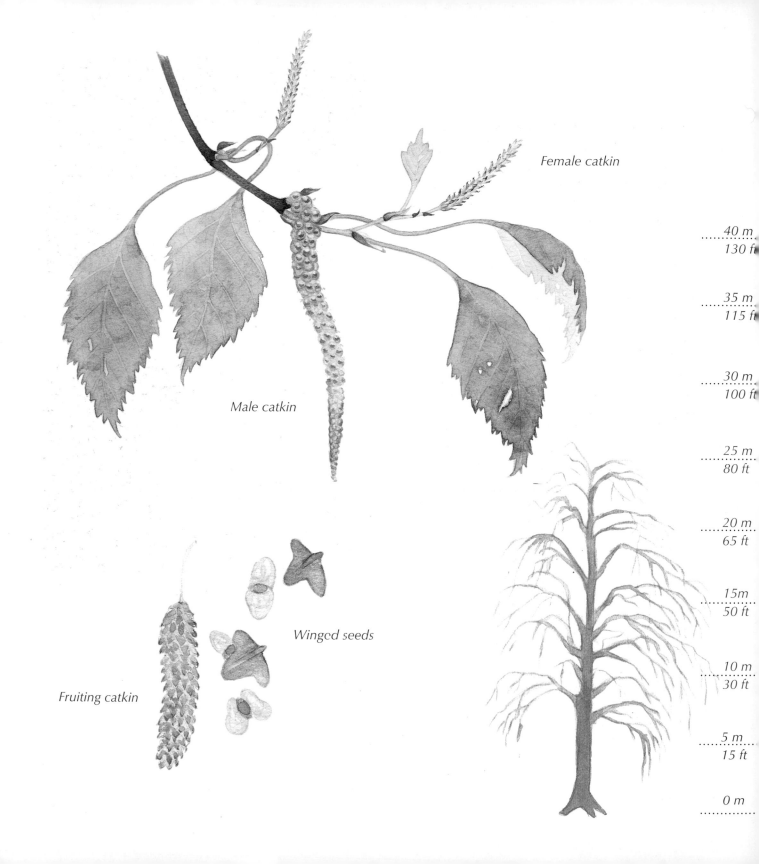

Female catkin

Male catkin

Winged seeds

Fruiting catkin

40 m
130 ft

35 m
115 ft

30 m
100 ft

25 m
80 ft

20 m
65 ft

15m
50 ft

10 m
30 ft

5 m
15 ft

0 m

Birch wood is suitable for making kitchen utensils such as bowls or spoons. Birch twigs are bound together to make brooms.

The leaves make a dye for wool and cloth. Depending on the strength of the dilution, the dye will give a yellow, green or grey colour.

A birch tree companion

There it stands all tall and beautifully grown in front of my window under the wide skies. For many years, in all kinds of weather, in the sunlight at dawn, in the red clouds at dusk; in spring in a dress of delicate leaves, in summer in rich green sheets of flowing foliage and then in autumn in a lovely golden outfit! Since I work by the window nearly all day long and also take my meals there, the birch is my nearest and best neighbour, my joy, a feast for my eyes.

(Heide Müller)

Letter written on birch-tree bark

Winking at us with its bark eyes

29

Spring

FOLKLORE

The birch tree plays an important part in the popular beliefs of many cultures – it is the tree of love and of good luck. It was thought to have protective powers against evil spirits: twigs hung up in the house were supposed to ward off lightning. People knew verses which they addressed to a birch to alleviate certain diseases. In some parts of the world cattle were driven to their pastures with birch switches because the twigs promised health and fertility.

When the fresh green of birches shows, it is a sign that winter has come to an end. The birch tree flowers early and with its delicate light green leaves effusing a balsamic scent it is a symbol for nature's renewing power. There are a number of spring customs around the birch tree, which mark the reawakening of nature.

The Maypole tradition

Various cultures had differing traditions regarding the first of May, depending on the state of the vegetation in the respective regions and on the imaginations and images used within the rituals of the individual tribes.

The Celtic people celebrated Beltane on the first of May: the Druids asked their goddesses for a good harvest and for many young and healthy animals. It was the custom in many areas to decorate streets, houses and special places with birch branches. On the first of May it was common for a birch tree to be cut in the woods, put up in the village square and decorated with coloured ribbons, paper garlands, eggs, biscuits and cakes. Using these symbols of reawakened nature, people asked for the blessing of the spring goddess. There was singing and dancing around the May birch. In some places young men placed a small birch tree or fresh green birch branches in front of the house of their beloved as a sign of their affection. Even today people celebrate the first of May. According to an old custom a May birch (nowadays often the trunk of a spruce tree) is decorated with ribbons and erected in the village square and there is a big neighbourhood get-together.

Making a gift for the goddess of spring

Tie a bunch of birch leaves onto a hazel switch. You can also use other newly 'awakening' twigs, buds or flowers. Decorate the greenery with ribbons. Place these spring poles in front of the house or in the garden as good-luck-wishes for the people living there. They also make a beautiful get-well present for sick people.

Leaves as spring food

Young finely chopped birch leaves are tasty in spring salads, soups and savoury cheese and yoghurt dishes.

Birch-bark love letters

Birch bark easily comes off felled trees in the form of papery strips. These bark strips used to be people's writing paper, so love letters written on this tree paper surely have a special effect. It's well worth trying it out (see p. 29)!

Summer

HOME REMEDIES

In spring and early summer the birch contains the largest amount of wholesome constituents. The birch can help regulate the lymphatic system. Tea prepared from birch leaves and birch-tree juice stimulate the bladder and the kidneys. Remedies made from birch-tree extracts are recommended for rheumatism, gout and skin diseases. Birch-leaf tea and birch-tree juice help us to retain our flexibility and vitality.

Birch-leaf tea

Infuse 1 teaspoon of birch leaves in a cup of hot water. Cover the cup and let it steep for 5 minutes, then strain. Birch-leaf tea has a wonderfully purifying effect on the body. Use as spring therapy and drink 2–3 cups daily over a period of 3 weeks.

Vitalising birch-tree juice

During some weeks in spring, birch-tree sap, which is rising within the trunk of the tree, can be tapped (ask the tree owners for permission). To collect the juice, drill a hole a few centimetres deep into the trunk at a height of 50–100 cm (1 1/2 – 3 1/4 ft). Insert a small glass tube. Collect the emerging sap in a container. In order not to damage the tree, only a few hundred millilitres (around 1/3 – 1/2 quart) should be taken. Then seal the hole well with tree wax. You can also cut a young branch and catch the juice dripping from it in a small container. Birch-tree elixir can also be purchased in health-food shops or chemists.

Drink one glass daily. Fresh birch-tree juice is very healthy and strengthens the body. It must be kept refrigerated. Birch-tree juice also used to be sold as a beauty drink.

Muscle oil

Put chopped bits of dried bark into a glass container and top with olive oil. Leave the glass in the sun for 2–3 weeks and then strain the mixture. Use birch-tree oil to treat muscle pain and rheumatoid diseases.

Massage oil

50 ml (1/4 cup) birch-tree oil (extract of birch-tree leaves and bark)
15 drops essential birch-tree oil

Put birch-tree leaves and/or bark bits into a glass container (until at least half full) and top with olive oil. Leave in the sun or near a radiator for 3 weeks. Add the essential birch-tree oil after straining.

This strengthening, vitalising massage oil is recommended for ailments such as rheumatism and muscle pain. You could also add some essential oil of juniper or rosemary.

Preparing a home remedy from birch leaves

Autumn

HAIR CARE

Hair-care products made with birch extracts are quite well known. You can buy birch shampoo and hair tonic. Birch products promote hair growth, are anti-dandruff and effective in treating greasy scalp problems. There are a few simple hair-care products that can be prepared at home using fresh leaves.

Birch-leaf hair conditioner
1 handful birch leaves
1/4 handful lavender blossoms
1/2 litre (1/2 quart) fruit vinegar
A little lavender essential oil

Pour the fruit vinegar over the birch leaves and lavender blossoms. Let the mixture steep for a few minutes, then strain. For a delicate fragrance, add some drops of lavender essential oil.

After washing the hair, massage the conditioner into the scalp. The hair will get lovely and shiny and the conditioner is effective against dandruff, hair loss, an itchy scalp or greasy hair. Do not use with light blonde hair since it may take on a slight green tinge.

Tree hair tonic
20 ml (4 tsp) birch-leaf tincture or birch-leaf vinegar
10 ml (2 tsp) calendula tincture or calendula vinegar
60 ml (1/4 cup) lavender water
A few drops of melissa (lemon balm) essential oil

To make the tinctures or vinegars, pour alcohol or vinegar over the plants in separate containers. Let them steep for a few minutes, then strain (see p.12). Now mix the tinctures or vinegar extracts together and add the essential oil of melissa in the mixture. Add the lavender water (prepared as tea, see p.11) and bottle the tonic.

Use to alleviate hair loss or an itchy or oily scalp. Apply a few drops to the scalp and massage lightly. Avoid contact with the eyes!

Winter

KEY SKILL: AGILITY, FLEXIBILITY AND LIGHTNESS

The birch's shape and gestures reveal a lot of its character and qualities. It epitomises youth and growth. It is light-filled, graceful, joyous and seemingly weightless. The agile leaves and slender twigs react to every breath of wind. The birch seems to deal with life in a playful manner. It shows what it can be like to be forgiving and transparent; the opposite of being unyielding and fixed. Flexibility is a key skill that is increasingly appreciated in many areas of life, particularly in the work place. The verb *flexere* originates in Latin and means 'to bend'. Something that can bend is flexible, able to adapt to various forms and situations. Flexibility as a concept means the ability to.

Adapt and change
Adjust to new situations and rethink
Change tasks
Work on various issues at the same time
Be open to new ideas

Drawing the birch

When striving to be flexible and mentally agile, we should try to adopt an open, playful manner. Sitting regularly under a birch tree can help us to do this. Observing a birch and drawing its basic gestures can help us to experience and understand flexibility and lightness.

Modelling trees

We can all learn from modelling trees out of clay. The instructions depend on the age of your group. Children can model trees and how they appear in the various seasons. Young people and adults can model four characteristic qualities of trees, such as:

Light, adaptable, flexible (birch)
Sturdy, self-confident, persevering (oak)
Cool, mediating (beech)
Cheerful, warm (sycamore)

Everyone receives a fist-sized lump of clay. During an agreed time of 5–10 minutes everybody works on their model, which is then put into the middle for all to see. Then the next task is worked on. The activity ends once all the seasons or characteristics have been modelled.

The task can reveal a lot about us and our attitudes. How difficult is it to adjust to a changing role? How flexible are we? What kind of solutions are found? What is the meaning of flexibility for each individual?

Modelling trees

Tree figures

3. Beech – Tree of Signs and Symbols

HABITAT AND CHARACTERISTICS

The beech has been living on Earth for a long time. It can be traced back to prehistory. Since they love a damp, cool climate, beech trees thrive in many parts of Europe and North America. They have smooth silvery bark and, especially in spring, delicate light-green leaves. We find beech trees growing in mixed forests as well as in beech woods. Had people not logged so many beech woods and later replaced them with plantations of spruce, Central Europe would still be covered with beech trees today. They may reach an age of 150–300 years. In summer the canopy of a beech tree is extremely dense. Small beeches don't mind the shade cast by their older relatives, but it is detrimental to young trees of different species.

ALL SORTS OF USES

Nowadays the beech tree has no great medical importance. In traditional medicine its bark, wood and fruit were used. The bark has astringent and anti-inflammatory properties. Tea prepared from the bark helps to lower fevers. Beech-wood ashes are effective as disinfectant. In the past, a cooling and anti-inflammatory poultice made with beech leaves was applied to the eye to treat eye styes. A paste made from beech-wood ashes and St John's wort oil was used to treat infected wounds of both humans and animals. Tea made from beech leaves served to cleanse slightly inflamed skin with enlarged pores.

People used to sleep on sacks filled with beech leaves as the scent has a calming effect. Beech leaves strewn onto the earth in autumn make a good blanket of mulch.

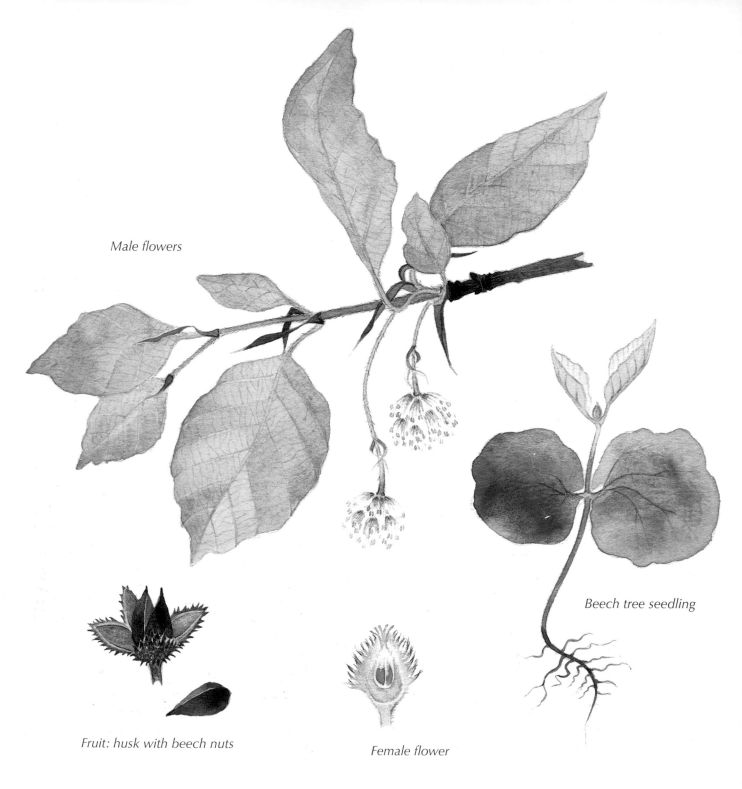

Male flowers

Beech tree seedling

Fruit: husk with beech nuts

Female flower

38

Spring

ANCIENT FOOD

Leaves: a delicacy

When the days start to lengthen, the buds of beech trees begin to stir and soon the leaves unfurl. The spring foliage of the beech is a delicate green and covered in silky hair. People used to eat beech leaves. The fresh or dried foliage was also fed to animals. Young beech leaves can even be steeped in alcohol and sugar to make beech liquor.

In spring, top your bread and butter with the fresh young leaves of beech, lime, birch, hawthorn, sycamore and hazelnut to create a delicious healthy snack. The leaves may also be mixed with salads and vegetables or added to soups and savoury cheese or yoghurt dishes.

Beech nuts: tree fruit for gourmets

In autumn, when the leaves are turning, the blossoms of spring will have become fruit and seeds. In 'mast years' (years when trees produce an abundance of fruit), three-cornered beech nuts cluster by their hundreds in the trees. Only in years when plenty of nuts are produced will enough seeds be left behind by foraging animals to start germinating.

Fresh beech nuts can be collected and eaten, although you shouldn't eat more than a few raw ones per day. They are very tasty when roasted in the oven (for 4–5 minutes at 100°C, 210°F). They lose their bitter taste and may then be eaten without concern; just as they are, or with yoghurt, in muesli or added to bread dough. Beech nuts store well when kept dry.

Beech-nut oil was popular, especially in times of need. It is a mild, long-lasting cooking oil, pressed from the peeled and ground nuts. 10 kg (22 lbs) of beech nuts make up to 1/2 litre (1/2 quart) of oil.

Beech nuts are also good for animals (poultry, goats and sheep) and can be mixed with other fodder. Pigs and goats used to be driven into beech woods to feed on the nuts.

Sandwiches with beech leaves and other natural ingredients

Summer

KEY SKILL: EXPRESSING YOURSELF

In olden times, the beech tree was closely interwoven with the daily lives of people in a variety of ways. This is even mirrored in today's language: members of the old Germanic tribes used to carve their runes into beech sticks to communicate. These original 'books' were made up of beechen boards with scratched pieces of writing on them. The Anglo Saxon word *bóc* originally meant 'beech tree'.

Even today, signs and letters are still carved into the bark of beeches. Hearts and initials of lovers remain visible for many years.

Rune sign language

Written messages can be scratched into small beech boards in the shape of simple 'runes'. We can scratch the symbols for 'protection' and 'strength' (oppostie) onto two beech sticks, put them into a small bag and carry them with us.
(From Nicola De Pulford, *Spells and Charms*)

A rune oracle

Over the course of many centuries the beech was thought to have prophetic properties. Beech sticks covered with magic symbols were used by wise men to predict the future. With the help of runes (from *runa* meaning secret) queries about life and future events were answered.

Chop a beech stick into equal parts, and mark each section with a symbol. Messages can also be written onto paper strips and glued to the bits of wood, such as: 'Express your opinion', 'Restrain yourself', 'Make somebody happy', 'Change a bad habit', 'Listen to the voice of the wind', 'Listen to your heart', 'Seek near the beech', 'Time to decide', 'The trees whisper the answer', 'There will be good news', 'Stay calm and think'.

Once you have thought of suitable messages, write them down and attach them to the sticks, then put the prepared sticks into a bowl. Now throw the runes onto a cloth and let everyone choose a stick. The message on each person's stick should indicate his or her own personal situation.

Experienced oracle readers take a few sticks and observe the order they were drawn, their spacing and interrelationship.

Making up stories about feelings

It's vital to be able to reflect on our situation, to be conscious of our feelings and bodies and to be able to express these perceptions. Feelings (joy, anger, enthusiasm, sadness etc.) are often communicated without words. Our gestures, facial expressions and body language show what we feel. It is essential to find words for our feelings too.

In a group, scratch or draw symbols for various feelings onto beech sticks. Mix up the beech sticks, and let each child choose a stick and tell a short story which fits that particular feeling. Then swap the sticks, and repeat the game at least three times.

Which were the 'easy' sticks? Which feelings were more difficult to express?

40 m
130 ft

35 m
115 ft

30 m
100 ft

25 m
80 ft

20 m
65 ft

15 m
50 ft

10 m
30 ft

5 m
15 ft

0 m

Strength

Protection

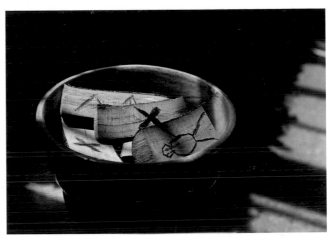

Sticks marked with symbols can inspire stories

Autumn

THROWING GAMES

There are countless games involving thrown dice or sticks in all sorts of variations the world over. Sometimes they were part of religious rituals; often they were just played for fun. Not only the dice we are familiar with, but carved bones and sticks were also played with. Throwing sticks is similar to the ritual of the oracle (see p.40), which uses sticks decorated with runes.

Throwing sticks are thin wooden sticks or boards (e.g. made of beech wood), decorated or painted on one side or in a different way on both sides. Patterns can also be burnt into the wood. All the sticks should be of a similar size.

Coloured throwing sticks
Preparation

You will need four sticks of a similar size, each squared off so it has four long, flat edges. You can also use bits of square timber or dowel. Paint one of the sides of each stick with the same colour. To count the score, collect pebbles, shells or pine cones (at least ten per player) and put them in a container.

Rules

One after the other, players throw the four sticks onto the ground. Then the points are counted according to the rules given below and the player gets that amount of pebbles.

2 painted, 2 unpainted sides = win 1 pebble
4 unpainted sides = win 2 pebbles
4 painted sides = win 3 pebbles
1 unpainted and 3 painted sides or 1 painted and 3 unpainted sides = lose 1 pebble (give it to the player with the least pebbles)

The first to get ten pebbles is the winner.

Native American game of throwing sticks
Preparation

You will need four flattish sticks. Draw or burn bands on one side of two of the sticks. Draw or burn one cross on one stick and five crosses on the fourth stick.

Rules

Throw the sticks onto the ground, then count the score:

3 marked sides, one unmarked side = 1 point
2 unmarked sides, 2 sides with bands = 3 points
2 unmarked sides, 2 sticks with crosses = 3 points
3 unmarked sides, 5 crosses = 4 points

All other options don't score any points. The winner is the first person to throw all the sticks with their marked sides showing, or the first to get 30 points.

Throwing sticks games

The prepared throwing sticks

Winter

BEECH WOOD

Beech wood is sturdy and durable and was therefore used to make items for daily use such as clothes pegs, bowls, toys and furniture. It's not suitable for building because it's not very elastic and not resistant to damp.

A warming fire

Beech wood has a high energy value, which is why it's excellent for burning. At one time it was widely used for charcoal burning and in glass production.

Well-seasoned beech wood is a good base for a fire. In all cultures and religions the fire was holy. It is a symbol of warmth and light. A fairy tale or story told by the fireside warms our hearts and souls.

Making soap

The large amounts of beech ash left over after a fire were used as washing suds.

To make beech-ash soap, pour lukewarm water over the beech ash and stir a few times. After a few hours strain the mixture through a closely woven cloth.

The suds made this way foam and clean just like soapsuds. Why not try washing some clothes in beech soap or perhaps cleaning the floor with them?

Beech ash was also applied to the fields as a fertilizer. And our great-grandparents still cleaned their teeth with wood ash.

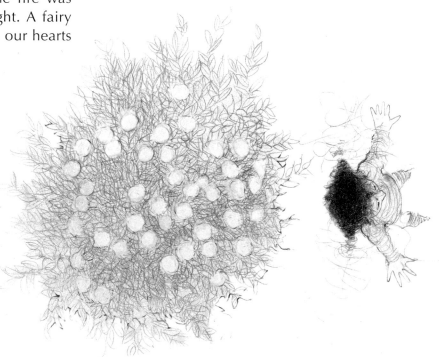

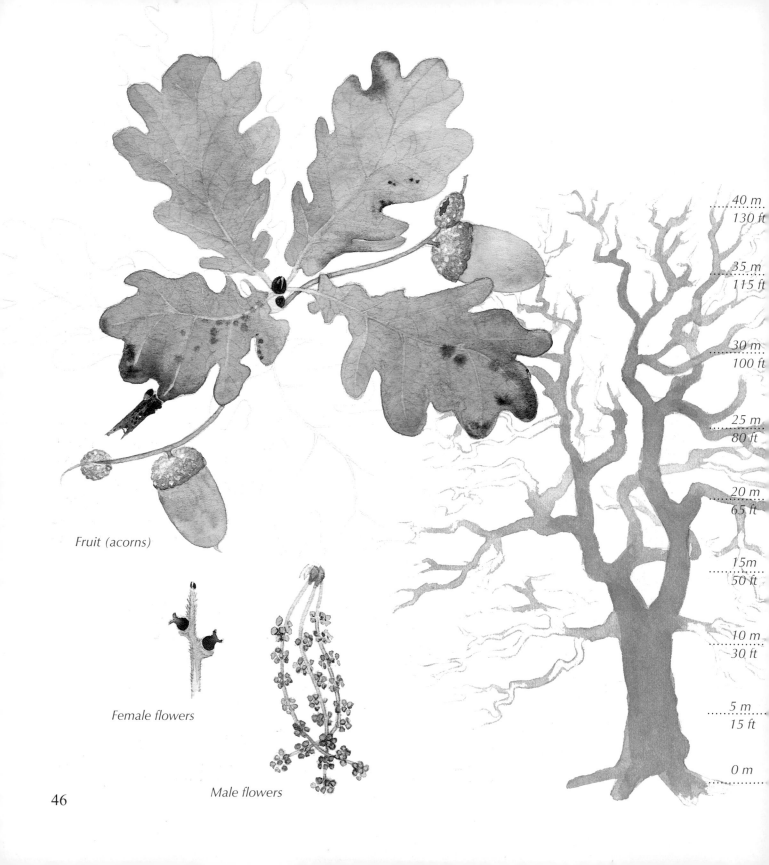

Fruit (acorns)

Female flowers

Male flowers

40 m
130 ft

35 m
115 ft

30 m
100 ft

25 m
80 ft

20 m
65 ft

15m
50 ft

10 m
30 ft

5 m
15 ft

0 m

46

4. Oak – Sacred Tree

HABITAT AND CHARACTERISTICS

Oaks grow throughout the northern hemisphere. A few centuries ago oak forests (as well as mixed oak and beech forests) still covered large parts of Central Europe. A mighty gnarled oak tree standing alone in a meadow or on a hill is a common sight. Oaks love deep, humus-rich soils. They like to take root in places where water veins cross, which is the reason why they are more prone to being hit by lightning than other trees.

ALL SORTS OF USES

Oaks had a prominent position in the daily lives of people and were highly esteemed in many different cultures. They often marked borders, too. They were meeting points and places of rest and often served as venues for trials or assemblies. The oak was also the namesake for some animals: oak hawk-moth, oak-gall wasp, oak titmouse. The oak is very popular due to its timber. Amongst the European timbers it is one of the hardest, most durable and most robust. It's even long lasting under water, so it was used for building ships, bridges and water wheels and also for making strong beams. Quality wine, whisky and sherry are still stored in oak casks today.

The corks used for stopping up wine bottles are made from the bark of cork oaks, which mainly grow in Portugal, Spain and Morocco.

The oak tree is also a source of medicinal and health products: its astringent properties are mainly due to the tannins in the leaves and bark. Oak bark gets peeled off the branches or the trunk (of felled trees) or you might be able to buy it in a pharmacy.

Footbath, washing lotion, gargle

Boil 2 tablespoons of oak bark in 1/2 litre (1/2 quart) of water for 15 minutes. Strain the water into a bowl. Used as a footbath this is effective against excessive sweating and cracked heels. Add it to your bath, use as washing lotion or gargle to treat eczema, boils, haemorrhoids, inflamed gums, enlarged glands and greasy skin. Do not take internally. Acorn coffee enhances the effect.

Spring

TREE SAPLINGS

The fully grown oak is a majestic tree with its mighty trunk and twisted branches. Just like any other living being it, too, starts quite small. In autumn the mother trees shed their seeds. most of which get eaten by rodents and birds during winter. Yet others hide under leaves and snow and wait for spring. When it starts to get warmer, the seeds awaken. They germinate and sprout their first leaves. If the seedling survives, it will grow into an oak tree over the course of decades. It will grow slowly but steadily, form deep roots and may get as tall as forty metres (130 feet). Only when it's about sixty years old will the oak flower for the first time. It can by far surpass the lifespan of a human being and become as old as 800–1000 years. Whoever plants oak trees does not only bear their own children in mind but also many future generations, indeed future itself.

Recognising the tree from its sapling?

It's like a miracle how with time tiny seeds and fruit grow into huge trees that may stand there for many centuries and generations. An apple tree grows from a small apple pip, a walnut tree slumbers in a walnut, the sycamore seed contains a sycamore tree, the chestnut a chestnut tree, from a beech nut a beech tree will grow, from an acorn an oak.

In spring, look for small tree saplings. Often the cotyledons (first leaves of saplings) have a different shape compared to the leaves of the fully grown tree. That's why it can be a bit of a detective job to recognise young trees. It will help to know the leaf shapes of the mature tree, and that most saplings don't grow far from the mother tree.

Planting trees

Planting a tree is a symbolic, life-embracing act. In autumn we can collect the seeds and fruit of trees. It's not easy to simulate the natural conditions of spring and encourage seeds to sprout, but it's worth trying!

In spring you can also look for a place outdoors where many saplings are growing. Carefully dig out one single sapling (without injuring the roots!) and plant it together with some of its surrounding soil into a plant pot at home. Place the pot in a sheltered place outside. When the sapling is about 10 cm (4 in) tall it can be planted outside – in your own garden or another piece of land after getting permission from the owner – remember that trees may get very big! You can also purchase young trees from tree nurseries.

The man who planted trees

The shepherd fetched a little bag and emptied a pile of acorns onto the table. Then he began carefully separating the good acorns from the bad. Once he had sorted out one hundred perfect acorns he stopped and went to bed. The next day the shepherd took the little bag of carefully chosen and counted-out acorns and dipped it into a bucket of water then off they went.

When they reached the place the shepherd was heading for, he began making holes in the ground with his iron rod and put an acorn into each hole. Then he covered the acorn with soil. He was planting oak trees...

(From Jean Giono, *The Man Who Planted Trees*)

Some seedlings will grow into mighty oaks

Summer

KEY SKILL: RESILIENCE, PERSEVERENCE, ASSERTIVENESS

The oak tree symbolises perseverance, sturdiness, self-confidence, strength, will power, resilience and assertiveness. Characteristics such as love of freedom, power and unbending pride tend to be associated with the oak, which is the reason why it is a feature of many coats of arms. Occasionally insignia are embroidered in the shape of oak leaves. Even today the winners of some boxing matches are honoured for their strength and perseverance with a wreath of oak leaves. The ancient Greek philosopher Socrates swore 'by the oak'. Marriage vows given under an oak tree were traditionally regarded as especially binding. Oak trees were also a popular place for court sittings and for carrying out sentences. The power of the oak becomes tangible when we contemplate the shape of this tree. It has angular, strong branches protruding from the stout trunk. Long tap roots searching for water deep down in the earth anchor the tree firmly in the ground.

The power tree
The oak is a strength-giving tree for human beings and animals alike. It was venerated by the ancient Germanic and Celtic people because of its vitality and old age. According to the Celtic calendar, people born on March 21 have special vitality and powers of endurance. An oak tree can help people lacking vitality to find new strength and power, so after long illnesses it's recommended to search out an oak. To feel its power one can sit underneath it, touch its trunk or hug it. The strength emanating from the oak is tangible. You can also carve a stick or a small fist-sized piece of oak wood, so the power and strength of the oak can accompany you through daily life.

Sensing the tree's energy

Oak meditation: 'I am like a strong tree'

The parts of the tree represent the conditions of human life:

The tree roots show us being rooted to a physical location. They symbolise what gives us strength. People can be firmly rooted or uprooted.

The mighty trunk is a symbol for sturdiness, resilience and self-confidence.

The bark protects the tree and the wood. It represents the sheltering cloak, the thick skin which helps to bear things easier.

The crown is the symbol for the ability to develop and to bear fruit – an image of the future, of vision and hope.

Either individually or in a group choose a straight, tall oak tree. Walk up to it, greet it, notice the sounds and scents in its vicinity and begin the meditation:

Imagine that you are the oak tree you have just looked at. You are as beautiful as the tree. You are also as old as the tree, as tall, as strong. With the help of energy, you grew from air, light, water and a little soil. Many human lives came and went and during all this time you only did one thing: you quietly continued to grow.

Thanks to your roots you stand firmly anchored in the ground. Your roots are branching out in all directions and have dug themselves deep into the earth. Your strong, stout trunk is striving towards the sky, *towards the light. The thick furrowed bark protects you. Your branches carry thousands of leaves constantly rustling in the wind.*

You grew over many summers. Many a storm has shaken you. In some winters the snow lay thickly on your branches. During many hundreds of nights the stars travelled above your head.

The oak – dwelling place of the gods, revered because of its old age and vitality

51

Autumn

FOOD FOR MAN AND BEAST

Trees offer many delicacies which can be processed with more or less effort: rose hips, beech nuts, elderberries, sea buckthorn berries, small nuts from spruce cones, hazelnuts, walnuts and acorns. The fruits of the oak, acorns, sit in hat-shaped cups. They are rich in carbohydrates and proteins.

Acorn mast

In times gone by the value of a forest was not only measured by its timber yield but also by its food yield. Pigs were turned loose in the forest to feed on the acorns. These nourishing fruit were their favourite. The years with plentiful acorns were called mast years. And later people were able to eat the delicious ham. There was even a saying in the Middle Ages: 'The best ham grows on oaks.'

For various reasons oak forests have strongly declined since the middle of the 16th century. Many forest areas were logged in order to gain arable land and to feed the growing population. With the advance of industrialisation the demand for wood – then the only source of energy – also increased. In addition, a lot of oak timber was used for ship building and for constructing railways.

An old 'bread tree'

For a long time, oaks also served as 'bread trees' for people. Foods such as acorn coffee or acorn flour were very common. With increasing supplies of food from foreign countries local products lost their value, however, and were just looked upon as poor people's food. Instead of acorn coffee people started to drink real coffee, ordinary tea or chocolate. Yet in times of need just a few decades ago, acorns were again made into acorn coffee, flour and bread.

Since acorns have a high tannin content they have to be de-bittered before being processed further into flour. The peeled, chopped fruit are boiled up a few times in water to wash out the tannins. It's important to change the water in between until the acorns have lost their bitter taste.

De-bittered, dried acorns are ground into flour, which can then be used to prepare both sweet and savoury dishes.

Acorn coffee

Crush the peeled acorns with a stone or hammer, brown them carefully in a hot frying pan and grind them into powder with a pestle and mortar. Keep in an airtight container.

For one cup of coffee, pour 1 cup of boiling water over 1 teaspoon of acorn powder. If you mix equal amounts of acorn coffee and hot milk or hot chocolate, it will taste even better (especially for children). You can also add some cinnamon. Acorn coffee is generally strengthening.

For quite some years now, tasty grain coffee has once again been available in the shops. Besides acorns the mixtures often include ingredients such as wheat, rye, barley, chicory and figs. This coffee substitute tastes good, it does not affect sleep and it may even be drunk by children.

In 'mast years' there were plenty of acorns to collect

Acorn cake

400–500 g (14 oz–1 lb) shortcrust pastry
200 g (7 oz) acorn paste (made with cooked
  acorns, margarine, olive oil, olives, onion,
  garlic and egg – see how to make below)
300 g (10 ½ oz) natural yoghurt
4 tablespoons honey
50 g (1 ¾ oz) raisins
100 ml (½ cup) milk
2 egg whites beaten stiffly
Cinnamon

Roll out the shortcrust pastry and line a baking tin.

To make the acorn paste, squash 250 g (9 oz) de-bittered (see page 52), cooked acorns and mix with 50 g (1 ¾ oz) margarine, 2 tablespoons olive oil, 75 g (2 ¾ oz) pitted olives, 1 finely chopped onion, 1 clove of crushed garlic and 2 egg yolks. Add salt to taste.

Mix 200 g (7 oz) of acorn paste with the yoghurt, honey, raisins and milk. Stir in the stiffened egg whites and add cinnamon.

Spread the acorn paste onto the shortcrust pastry and bake at a medium heat setting for half an hour.

(From: Francois Couplan, *Wildpflanzen für die Küche*).

Winter

SACRED TREE

The oak has always been venerated for its vitality and old age. For our Germanic and Celtic ancestors, as well as for many other cultures, the oak was sacred and dedicated to the gods. With some people it was customary to honour their deities by lighting oak fires which were kept burning for the whole year. Young women threw wreaths of oak leaves into the trees. If a wreath got caught on a branch, this was taken as an omen for a wedding in the near future. Zeus, the father of the Greek gods, always wore a wreath of oak leaves on his head.

With the Romans, too, the oak was sanctified and dedicated to Jupiter. For the Germanic people the oak was the tree of Donar, the god of thunder.

For many centuries the church associated oak trees with heathen ideas, devils and witches, a fact which often led to old oak trees being felled. But the knowledge and belief in the power of these trees was never completely extinguished.

Druids and mistletoe

The Celts, too, revered oaks as sacred trees and felt themselves strongly connected with them. Their kings held counsel beneath oak trees. The spiritual Celtic leaders were called Druids, which means 'the ones who have knowledge about oaks'. During their years of preparation, trainee wise men studied and meditated in oak groves before working as Druids. They also celebrated their rituals there. Anything growing on oaks was sacred to the Celts – particularly mistletoe harvested from oak trees, which they believed was endowed with secret powers and was revered as the all-healing herb.

Medicinally, mistletoe was mainly used to make remedies that lower the blood pressure.

Mistletoe plants are evergreen shrub-like, semi-parasitic plants, which live in symbiosis with oaks.

In winter, mistletoe plants are easily recognisable in the tops of trees. They also grow on other deciduous trees and conifers. The white berries with their sticky juice get transferred by birds to other trees, where they germinate and sprout. Mistletoe mainly lives off the nutrients and water of the host tree.

Mistletoe is mentioned in many old tales and myths. Apparently the Celtic Druids dressed all in white when they cut mistletoe with golden sickles in the moonshine. According to popular folklore mistletoe twigs are hung above the door or inside houses at Christmas time to ward off evil spirits and to attract good luck. In the UK everyone knows that you are allowed to kiss someone standing under the mistletoe.

Making a mistletoe amulet

Fasten a small twig of mistletoe to a length of leather or string. Wear this amulet around the neck to protect against illness and misfortune the whole year round. Even today a mistletoe amulet can be something quite enchanting.

Making a magic bag

Collect any attractive natural objects: mistletoe twigs, pieces of wood or bark, herbs, fruit, stones etc. Place the collected items in a piece of fabric and fasten with a piece of string or leather.

These magic bags serve as charms. Keep the bag in a secret place so that good luck remains with you. A smaller bag can also be worn around the neck.

A magic bag and mistletoe amulets empower and protect

Asterix and Obelix

The stories of *Asterix and Obelix* are full of old Celtic heritage. The oak plays an important part as an ingredient in a magic potion. The Druid Miraculix used acorn extract, wormwood, southernwood, St John's wort, a pinch of agaric, a drop of hen bane and many other things to mix his famous strength-giving magic potion; ever since Obelix fell into the cauldron containing the magic potion he has been invincibly strong.

Mistletoe – fruit and flowers

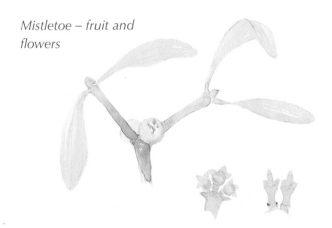

Who would not wish for a bottle of magic potion now and again?

55

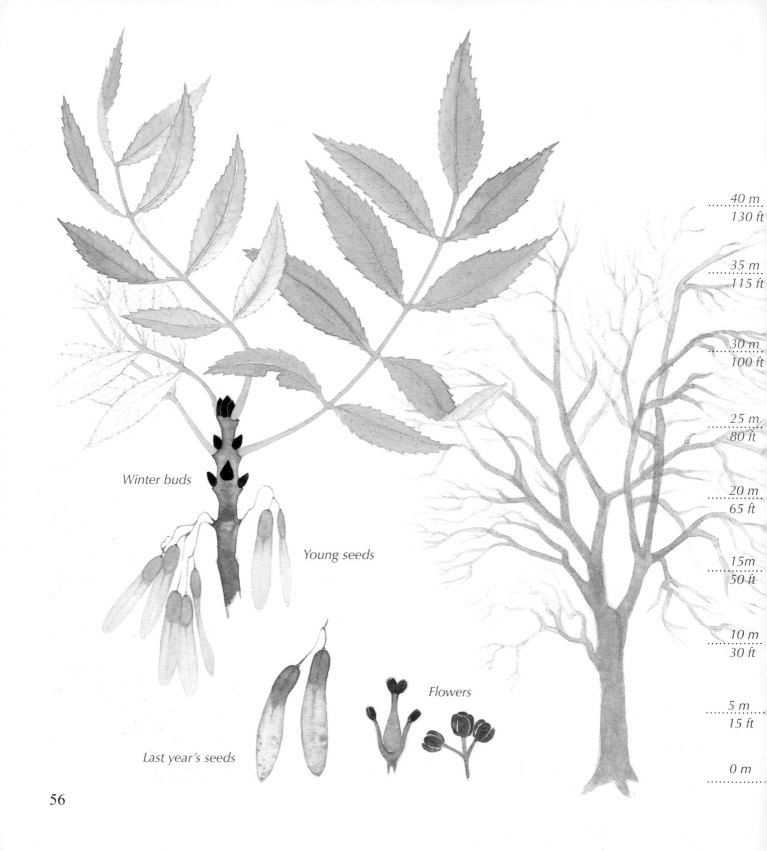

Winter buds

Young seeds

Last year's seeds

Flowers

40 m
130 ft

35 m
115 ft

30 m
100 ft

25 m
80 ft

20 m
65 ft

15m
50 ft

10 m
30 ft

5 m
15 ft

0 m

56

5. Ash – Tree of Life

HABITAT AND CHARACTERISTICS

The ash is one of the mightiest native trees. It can grow as tall as 40 metres (130 ft) and its root system is so extensive it can spread within a radius of up to 100 metres (328 ft). Ash trees can reach 250 years old and they are common throughout the northern hemisphere.

The seeds of the ash tree grow in distinct dense bunches and they usually remain hanging on the tree during winter. Since the ash is very sensitive to frost, its leaves appear later in spring than those of other trees. The ash is an 'energy thief': it exhausts the soil in its vicinity because it needs a lot of energy itself. It's not possible to use poles made from ash wood to support other plants, as the plants either die off or try to evade the pole.

ALL SORTS OF USES

In traditional agriculture ash leaves were used as animal bedding and feed, which is the reason why ash trees were often planted near farms. The ash was cut and kept small with billhooks (a type of knife). The branches were tied together and dried in the shed for use in winter. Ash leaves were given to sick animals and occasionally they were used as filling for mattresses and quilts.

The young sticky leaves can be eaten in salads and it's possible to extract oil from the ripe seeds.

Ash timber is hard, durable and yet elastic, so it can take a lot of stress.

This is why ash timber has long been used for making wooden wheels, ladders and handles for tools. For a long time, people also used ash to make sports equipment, such as tennis rackets, skis and bars, as well as walking sticks. Ever since antiquity ash wood has been used for making weapons such as crossbows, spears, lances and bows. According to Greek mythology, Chiron – a being half man half horse – made an ash wood spear for Achilles who later used it to win victory.

Ash timber has a very beautiful grain pattern and is therefore popular for furniture making.

Spring

GAMES USING ASH WOOD

Throwing games and games with hoops are traditional all over the world, and in some places they are regaining their popularity.

The basic rules tend to be quite simple – they can also be slightly adjusted or re-invented. Throwing games mostly test agility and accuracy. They are all about challenge, self-assertiveness and having fun.

Spears

Spears are often made from ash wood, and sometimes also from willow. You can decorate the shafts in various ways. Peel off parts of the bark, then hold the shaft over a fire until the peeled areas are blackened. To finish, peel off the remaining bark.

Ring-toss games

You can make supple, thin ash or willow twigs into rings, especially in spring. After bending the twigs to form a ring they are tied with string. Throw the ring through the air to friends, or try to hoop the ring over a stick. You can also put sticks into the ground at various distances over which the rings have to be tossed. The players who can reach the furthest sticks, get the highest points.

Games with hoops require little preparation and can be played anywhere

Hoop game

Using the same method as described above, hoops can be made from ash or willow rods. Fill the inside of the hoop by criss-crossing it with string like a spider's web. One person throws or rolls the hoop while another aims a stick or arrow at it to win points.

Opposite: Spears, bows and arrows have been made from ash since antiquity

Summer

The magic tree

If you look closely, you can see a strange creature peeping out from the tree late in the afternoons. The air is clear and the young elf dances out into the balmy summer evening. In the distance she hears somebody crying quietly. Is it the small boy again who lives in the wooden hut beneath the ash tree? The elf flies a bit closer and, indeed, there's the boy sitting in front of his grandfather's hut crying his heart out. Beside him on the ground is a big empty sack. When the elf appears in front of him the boy gets a fright. But then he recognises his former playmate. He tells her why he's so sad and asks for her help. His grandfather is very sick, with pains in his arms and legs, and he can barely move. The boy is at a loss how to help his grandfather. And he's scared of walking on his own all the way to the village to get the messages.

The elf replies cheerily, 'Nothing simpler than that! Your help is just above your home. Your ash tree will help you. Listen to the rustling of the leaves and you will get new hope. Then take some ash leaves and mix them with the leaves of the stinging nettle and make some tea for your old grandfather. Brew three cups of tea for him every day. And place a few ash leaves into your own shoes, then your feet won't get tired walking the long way to the village.'

So the boy set out. Once he tripped over a stone and cut his leg. The only thing he had at hand to stop the bleeding was a bit of bark from the ash tree. And lo and behold, the wound stopped bleeding straight away.

He was not afraid of the snakes in the forest, for in his bag he was carrying a mixture of leaves, bark and roots of the ash to ward them off.

And when he did return home, after not too long, he brewed tea from ash leaves for his grandfather. This made the grandfather smile. He knew a secret recipe with ash seeds that he had learned as a child; prepared as tea, they were supposed to enhance the powers of love... In any case, the grandfather soon was better. It is truly magic, this ash, a tree of love and healing.

HEALTH PRODUCTS AND HOME REMEDIES

The ash used to be highly esteemed as a heal-all remedy. Even today the leaves and seeds are used to treat gout and rheumatism. The seeds are thought to have a diuretic and blood-purifying effect. There are also treatments which alleviate pain and lower fevers. In some areas the ash tree was called the tree of healing. In order to stop wounds from bleeding, strips of ash bark were applied to the injured areas.

There are countless other traditional remedies using parts of the ash tree. The seeds prepared as tea are supposed to enhance the powers of love. Ash leaves placed in shoes help with tired feet. It was generally known that the ash was an antidote to snake poison. It is said that if in danger, snakes rather seek out fire than the leaves of an ash. And last but not least people used to listen to the rustling of ash leaves to foretell the future.

The leaves are collected in early summer, the seeds in autumn.

Autumn

KEY SKILL: CREATIVITY AND PROBLEM-SOLVING

Creativity and problem-solving skills are much in demand nowadays and they do make life easier. The ash tree can help and support us in nurturing these qualities.

Creativity is the ability to approach things in a new and original way, to look at problems in a different light and to find solutions that differ from the usual thought patterns. To achieve this, we need ingenuity and to be inventive.

Creative people have active imaginations. They are not overly quick in criticising others but are open to new ideas. They are prepared to take risks and are curious to learn new things. The seeds of creativity lie in all of us, and they can be encouraged to grow by learning new modes of thought and action.

The character of the ash has an invigorating and strengthening effect and it stimulates the imagination. The ash tree helps when people have become set in their ways or are having to cope with disappointments. Just spending regular periods of time near an ash tree can be of help and support.

Magic wands

The Celtic Druids made their magic wands from ash wood. The ash has a connection with water. In times of drought, rain can apparently be conjured up with the help of a magic wand made of ash wood. Try carving and decorating a magic wand from ash wood, using your imagination.

Imaginative journeys

Going on an imaginative journey can open our imaginations and enhance our creativity. It's also a relaxing activity, and the instructions can be spoken over quiet music playing in the background. One person is assigned the part of the speaker. Below are a few ideas, which always begin with: 'Imagine you are...'

Magic wands. Will my wish come true?

You could imagine you are a tree, and focus on the development and life of a tree: fruit, seeds, roots, cotyledons, first branches, growing into the depths of the earth, forming its annual rings, old branches breaking, building a wooden hut beneath the tree, your hundredth birthday etc.

Or you could observe the tree during the course of the year: in spring imagine your leaves unfurling and buds growing, leaves changing colour and falling off in autumn etc.; imagine the weather through the seasons: nightly frost, rain, sunshine, thunder and lightning, getting shaken by the wind, the weight of the snow, a woodpecker hammering a hole, the change from day to night etc.

Dreamscapes

Daydreaming stimulates the imagination. Try inventing a landscape you would like to live in. What do your surroundings have to be like to make you feel happy? Create your landscape using natural objects.

Winter

THE TREE AS SYMBOL OF LIFE AND THE ORIGIN OF MAN

Many cultures designated certain trees as 'trees of life'. These could be ash trees, spruces, yews, elm trees or oaks. The tree of life is the centre and symbol of life. It connects the world of the gods, the underworld and the world of human beings. It harbours all wisdom and knowledge. It is said that some of the great teachers of mankind attained enlightenment beneath trees.

In the creation stories of many religions 'trees of life' are described. The tree grows up from its roots, reaching deep into the earth. The branches continue from the trunk and in turn the leaves, needles, flowers and fruit grow from the branches and twigs. Everything is connected with everything else. The darkness of the earth is lifted up to the light of the sky. The leaves and flowers direct the light back down to the earth. The tree has often been admired and revered because it grows upwards and downwards at the same time.

The gesture of a tree with its trunk and spreading branches is similar to that of a human being. In some mythologies the first human couple is born from a tree. In others, it is said that the first human beings were created from the wood of a tree.

Yggdrasil, the World Tree

In the creation story of the ancient Germanic people the tree of life was an ash tree. The *Edda*, a collection of epic poems and stories of the Norse gods, describes the world ash tree Yggdrasil. People imagined that their whole world had the shape of a huge tree growing in the middle of the world, forming its axis and support. This tree connected all areas of life: the underworld – Nilfheim; the land of the giants – Jötunheim; and Asgard – the city of the gods. The crown of the tree was connected with the heavens. The realm of human beings was beneath it. Below the earth were the roots and in this underworld lived the three Norns, the goddesses of destiny. It was their task to water the roots and to weave the threads of destiny that determined the lives of human beings. The world tree was also home to mystical animals; it was guarded by an eagle, and squirrels

Representing a tree from roots to trunk to leaves

nested in its branches. Deer and goats ate its leaves. Every day the gods came to visit the world tree via the rainbow and, sitting in its shade, they passed judgement on mankind.

Human tree game

You can make a game out of representing a tree, in which the group members act out various parts of the tree: roots, heartwood (the inner wood of the trunk), sapwood (the outer, living wood) the bark, branches and leaves. A game leader gives instructions for the individual tasks.

The first three players stand back to back in the centre. They represent the heartwood, giving strength and support to the tree. They are big and strong and are told to join hands.

Four to five players lie on the ground around the trunk, forming the roots that anchor the tree. Their hair symbolises the finest roots. The 'roots'

suck water and trace elements from the soil by making slurping noises.

At least six players stand around the heartwood, facing in – they are the outer layer of wood on the trunk, the sapwood, in which the sap flows. Inside them water rises up to the branches, twigs and leaves, which are represented by arms, hands and wiggling fingers. To show the sap rising, the players kneel and then they rise upwards making slurping 'sap-conducting' noises.

The 'nourishment' produced in the leaves with the help of sunlight is transported to all the other parts of the tree. The players again kneel down and share out the 'food' with a suitable sound.

Finally, the rest of the players represent the bark. They stand, facing outwards and join hands. They protect the tree by making faces to scare away potential aggressors.

(From Joseph Cornell, *Sharing Nature With Children*)

Our ancestors revered trees, which is clear from mythology, religion and folklore

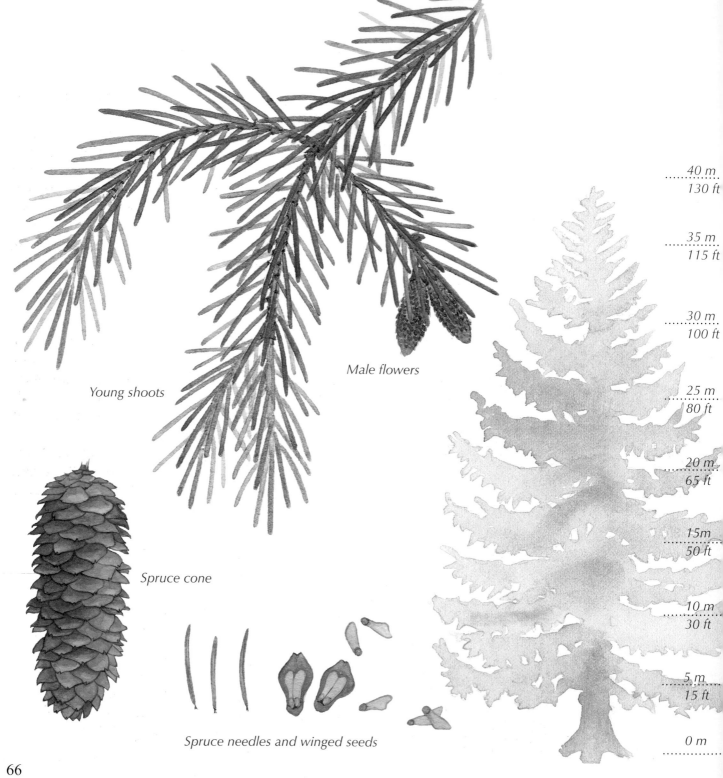

Young shoots

Male flowers

Spruce cone

Spruce needles and winged seeds

40 m
130 ft

35 m
115 ft

30 m
100 ft

25 m
80 ft

20 m
65 ft

15m
50 ft

10 m
30 ft

5 m
15 ft

0 m

6. Spruce – Tree of Light

HABITAT AND CHARACTERISTICS

Standing on its own, a spruce may grow into a striking tree. Its trunk is straight and the branching pattern regular. Spruce trees are amongst the tallest European trees.

Spruces originate in uplands and mountainous areas. Today they are also found at lower altitudes, in bogs and alluvial forests where their seeds are deposited.

People often confuse spruces (latin, *Picea*) with fir trees (latin, *Abies*). They are closely related and their medicinal properties are similar too. Obvious signs of distinction are their cones: spruce cones hang down from the branches, whereas fir cones stand upright. For the last 200 years spruce trees have been growing in all areas and altitudes. During the industrial revolution with its demands for energy, deciduous forests were often clear felled, leading to a timber shortage. As a reaction to this catastrophic loss of forests, people began to reforest vast areas with spruces because they are particularly fast growing trees. Even today, man-made spruce forests dominate the countryside in many regions. Disadvantages of the proliferation of just one tree type are the acidification of the soil and an increased danger of pest attacks. Nowadays, deciduous trees are planted together with spruce and fir trees again, since mixed forests are more ecologically sound, have greater resilience and are just as economically viable.

ALL SORTS OF USES

Spruce trees yield large quantities of timber, which is excellent for construction, furniture making and fuel. Because of its high resin content, fresh or dried spruce wood is highly flammable. Spruce timber is also largely used for paper production.

Spruce is also known as 'violin wood'. Before making his famous violins, the violin maker Stradivari personally chose the best spruces in the Alps.

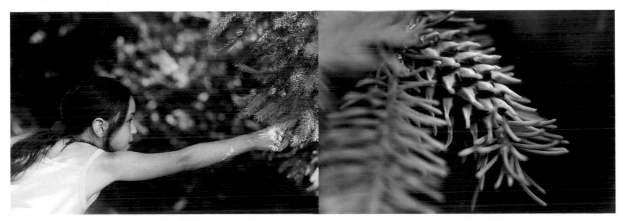

Spring

HEALTH PRODUCTS

Even Stone-Age man knew the healing properties of the spruce. It was particularly recommended to treat coughs, colds and rheumatism. The scent of spruce trees was used as a medieval remedy to try and halt epidemics. In herbalism, it's mainly the needles and resin that are important. Young tips are collected in spring from the lower branches only. Neither the upper branches nor their tips are ever taken. You will need permission to collect larger quantities.

Spruce-needle tea

Cook 1 teaspoon of young spruce needles in 1 cup of water on a low heat for 15 minutes, then strain.

This tea is strengthening and refreshing, it can help colds, coughs, flu, kidney and bladder infections, chronic skin diseases and you can drink it regularly as a spring detox. Drink 4–5 cups daily. Herbal mixtures often contain spruce buds. They go well with peppermint leaves, lemon balm and calendula flowers.

Spruce-needle syrup

Boil 5 handfuls of fresh needle buds in 1 litre (1 quart) of water. After straining, add 1 kg (2 lb) of sugar to the fluid and boil it down to syrup or honey consistency. Then pour into jars.

Spruce-needle syrup relieves coughs and colds.

Spruce-resin ointment

Many tribal people still use resin ointments today. In the West these are only used officially in veterinary practice – yet they are well worth rediscovering.

Resin has a warming effect as well as wound-healing and disinfecting properties. It's used to treat wounds, diseases of the respiratory system (e.g. sinusitis) and rheumatism.

10 g (1/3 oz) spruce resin (collected in the wild or bought as raw material for cosmetics production)
50 g (1 3/4 oz) olive oil
1 handful ribwort plantain, calendula or other herbs suitable for treating wounds or colds
5 g (1/5 oz) beeswax
12 drops essential oil
Small containers (such as empty plastic medicine or vitamin pots)

Warm the resin until fluid, then pour the olive oil over it. Mix in the herbs and let it steep for 2–3 hours. Strain and melt the beeswax in this warm mixture. Before bottling, put the essential oil into the small containers. Only close them up when the ointment has completely cooled down.

Other uses

An inhalation with spruce needles helps sinusitis and lung problems.

A tincture of fresh spruce buds is recommended as liniment for rheumatism, gout and lumbago.

Fresh young tips of fir are delicious in spring salads or soups. They are rich in vitamin C. In the Middle Ages people even brewed fir-tree beer.

Young spruce shoots can be made into a variety of natural products

Summer

KEY SKILL: RELAXATION, MOTIVATION AND BALANCE

The constantly changing demands on our time, the many possibilities presented to us, our ever increasing mobility, the fast pace at school, in the workplace and during leisure time – all create symptoms of stress. Stress has a negative effect on health and lowers people's efficiency.

The spruce can alleviate symptoms of nervousness, tension and restlessness. It has a cooling effect and calms and restores balance, even in easily agitated people. Even if we just spend a little time near a spruce tree (a lone spruce would be best), we will be able to feel its benefits.

Incense made from spruce needles is also effective in treating nervousness, stress and anxiety. One's worries will evaporate with the smoke (see p. 73).

CALMING TREATS
Spruce-needle bath

Taking a spruce-needle bath is generally strengthening; above all it calms the nerves and will relieve exhaustion. In addition, it stimulates circulation, has expectorant properties and may alleviate rheumatism and skin rashes.

Many bath additives made with spruce needles are available to buy, but you can easily make some yourself as well: pour 1 litre (1 quart) of boiling water over 2 handfuls of spruce needles and let the mixture steep for 15 minutes. Strain and add to bath water.

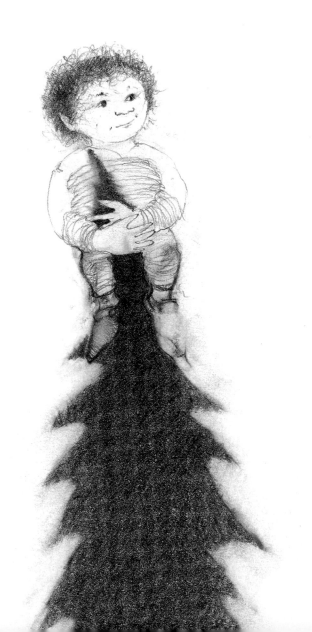

70

Refreshing body oil

1 handful spruce needles
50 ml (1 2/3 fl oz) almond or olive oil
10–12 drops essential oil of spruce or fir cones

In a sunny place, let the spruce needles steep in the oil for 3 weeks. Shake occasionally. Strain and add the essential oil.

The scent of spruce can strengthen and enliven us if we're feeling weak and tired. It gives fresh hope and encourages more positive and cheerful thoughts and feelings.

Fitness oil

Crush spruce needles in a bowl. Pour some almond oil over them and let the mixture steep in the sun for 3 weeks. After straining, add essential oil of rosemary or lavender. Use as body oil.

Fragrant oil burner

Burning spruce essential oil in a ready-made oil burner has a calming, harmonising, strengthening and refreshing effect. The fragrance of spruce transforms inner restlessness, nervousness and tension into a state of peace and balance. Essential oil of spruce is also invigorating for the lungs, cleanses and helps to breathe more deeply.

Spruce-needle pillow

A small pillow filled with young dried spruce needles promotes sleep, and calms and strengthens the nerves. Simply fill a small cloth bag with the dried needles.

Spruce needles steeped in oil are ready for further processing after three weeks

Autumn

MAKING INCENSE

In all ancient cultures burning incense was an important ritual in people's daily lives. Even today in many eastern countries the use of incense is an essential part of celebrations and daily tasks. We can rediscover the supportive benefits of incense by including small rituals in our daily routine.

When creating incense, aromatic substances are burnt up in the embers of a fire, on hot stones or on charcoal. Incense vessels can be made from clay, stone, metal or porcelain. For burning incense in the open, it works best to put the substances onto hot flat stones by the fireside. If plant material is put directly into the flames, it tends to burn too quickly and hardly develops any scent. At home the substances may be placed on a glowing piece of wood in the fireplace. Incense material is mainly of plant origin: leaves, blossoms, seeds, fruit, resin, wood. It must always be well dried when burned. Fan the scent towards yourself with a feather. Incense affects the senses in various ways. It helps with relaxation, meditation, encourages creativity and gives strength and courage.

Natural incense from spruce needles, resin and wood

The needles and resin of spruce are well suited for making incense and both develop a similar fragrance. They probably belong amongst the oldest incense materials used in Europe. Over time, more exotic incense became popular and spruce lost its importance.

Needles: spruce branches burning in a fire diffuse a pleasant scent of pine forests. For incense mixtures, dried spruce needles are most suitable. To prepare them, pluck the needles off the twigs and dry in a shady place. When dried, keep the needles in an airtight container so the scent doesn't evaporate. Later on, crush the dried needles or grind them with a pestle and mortar. You can also add this powder to various incense mixtures. Spruce needles go well with frankincense or mastic resin. Incense containing spruce is refreshing; it cleanses the atmosphere and is disinfecting.

Resin: if the tree's bark or wood gets injured, it will react with resin flow. Summer is the best season to collect resin, as the water content of the tree is at its highest because of evaporation processes in the tree. Resin should be stored for about a year before being used as incense, then it will diffuse a pleasant sweet-balsamic scent. Resin can be very smoky when burned, so it's advisable to use this substance as incense outdoors. Creating incense with spruce resin is thought

to protect from disturbing influences and to restore calm. Spruce resin kills bacteria, a quality which enables it to disinfect the air. That's why people used to burn spruce resin in sick rooms. It was also recommended for treating rheumatism and to clear mucus from the lungs.

Wood: spruce and fir-wood incense cleanse closed rooms and keep disruptive elements away. Similar to using resin or needles, the wood has a warming, protective and comforting effect.

Tree incense

Below is a list of various parts of trees that can be used to make incense:

Beech wood (or beech-wood shavings)
Oak moss (the greyish growth on oak trunks)
Ash seeds
Spruce needles, resin and wood
Hazel bark
Elderflower blossoms, pith, wood and bark
Lime bark
Bay leaves
Mistletoe
Cloves
Sandalwood
Juniper berries and twigs
Sloe blossoms
Cedar wood
Cinnamon bark
Cypress

These tree products are often mixed with dried sage, coriander seeds, thyme, hyssop, star anise, mugwort or mastic resin. Mastic is obtained from a Greek tree and it reinforces the scent of the other incense ingredients.

Winter

THE TREE OF RETURNING LIGHT

The cycle of the year ends on December 21, the darkest time of year. From then on, the hours of light will increase again, the days get longer and the sun regains its strength. With the winter solstice we celebrate the rebirth of light.

The trees that do not shed their greenery in winter have always represented good luck and the return of light and life. Spruce and fir trees are seen as trees of life. Their evergreen twigs are used for window decoration and made into wreaths. The custom of decorating a fir or spruce tree and putting it up after the winter solstice at Christmas time is not very old. Initially only the well-to-do citizens had a Christmas tree and it was only in the 19th century that this custom was taken up by poorer folk.

The trees were decorated with red and golden apples and nuts, which, too, are a symbol of fertility and renewal. The Christmas tree stands for wealth and good luck. Over time, the apples were exchanged for shiny baubles. The trees are also adorned with light-giving candles.

A midwinter celebration

On the night before December 21, close to midnight, choose a tree in a wood or garden and start walking towards it, without a light to show the way. When you arrive at your chosen tree, light candles or torches, and let the light illuminate the darkness; by doing this, the new light becomes a real experience. Then you can light a fire and sing songs. The tree can be decorated with natural materials: apples, nuts, etc. Later, on your way home, everyone can carry a burning candle. Darkness becomes light.

Natural windcharms

Drill holes into various natural materials (spruce cones, chestnuts, snail shells, seashells, stones, nutshells), using an awl or a drill. Thread the items onto a piece of string and tie to a branch. You will be able to hear the fine music of the wind.

Christmas incense

1 part fir resin
2 parts fir needles
1 part juniper berries
3 parts mastic resin

Crush the dry resin, the bark and the needles in a mortar or cut the ingredients. Squash the juniper berries and mix everything together. Burn the incense in the fire, on hot stones or on charcoal.

(From Susanne Fischer-Rizzi, *The Complete Incense Book*)

Winter stories

Many fairy tales and legends are set in old fir forests and are about fir trees. One of Hans Christian Andersen's less well-known stories is called *The Fir Tree*. The story is about a little fir tree who is desperate to grow up and wishes for a more exciting life. Finally it ends up as a Christmas tree in a rich family's house. Has it really found happiness?

Tree candles shine mysteriously into the night

Female
flowers

Male flowers

40 m
130 ft

35 m
115 ft

30 m
100 ft

25 m
80 ft

20 m
65 ft

15m
50 ft

10 m
30 ft

5 m
15 ft

0 m

7. Hazel – Magic Tree

HABITAT AND CHARACTERISTICS

The hazel is common throughout the northern hemisphere. It's not a very demanding tree and likes slightly damp soil. After the last Ice Age the hazel found the best of conditions, and over the course of many centuries Central European landscapes were dominated by huge hazel woods. Today, individual hazel bushes grow at the edge of forests, in hedges and gardens.

Hazels make excellent hedging plants for the garden, behind which the wilderness of legends and fairy tales was created – populated by scary ogres and other spirits. In folklore, only herbalists and magicians dared to venture beyond these 'magic' hedges.

ALL SORTS OF USES

The hazel flowers in February. Its catkins, together with dried elderflower blossoms, can be infused in early spring to make a tea that can reduce fever symptoms in flu sufferers and induce perspiration.

The wood is elastic and tough. It is used in carpentry and wood turning, for making walking sticks, toys and many other things.

Hazelnuts are very popular and widely used in food, particularly in sweet dishes and confectionary.

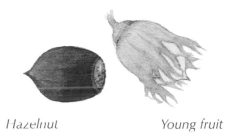

Hazelnut   *Young fruit*

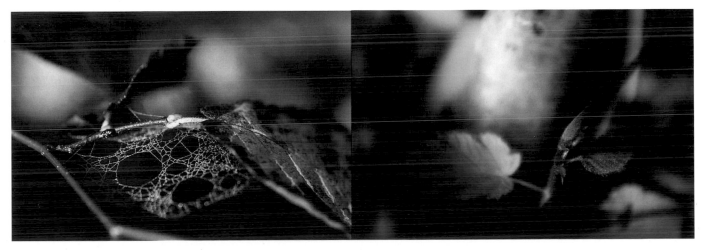

Spring

MAGIC POWERS

Hazel wood has energy conducting properties. It serves as a dowsing rod to search for underground water veins, indicated by positive or negative energy fields. In the past, people used dowsing rods to discover hidden treasures, too. According to some popular legends, golden keys to treasure chests can be found hanging in the hazel bush. Maybe the hazel can fulfil our secret wishes?

The hazel bush is deeply rooted in our culture. Just like the elderflower, it is supposed to have protective qualities and keep fires, snakes, diseases and enchantments away. Many people believe that the hazel can help us to contact nature spirits. Because of it's lightning conducting properties, hazel rods used to be fastened in front of windows and doors before a thunderstorm or they were put in the field. Farmers protected themselves by adorning their hats with a hazel twig.

Celtic judges used hazel rods during their court hearings and priests foretold the future with their help. During peace talks people often held hazel switches in their hands to show their good intentions. Even magic wands were made from hazel wood. Hazel rods also served to conjure up rain, but also to calm thunderstorms.

Talking stick

For centuries, Native American tribes used a 'talking stick' during meetings, which allowed all members of the group the opportunity to explain their point of view. The talking stick was passed around and only the person holding it was allowed to speak. The others listened without criticism or comment. The stick was only passed on when the speaker posed a question to someone or had finished his or her contribution.

This way of discussing things emphasises the individual and his or her opinion. Everyone listens to the speaker, so nothing has to be repeated. Naturally discussion and disagreements were allowed, but each person truly had a chance to contribute to the decision-making process.

The talking stick can teach us to honour the values and opinion of every living creature. It teaches us how to listen to each other and to treat what we have heard with respect. It shows us that life has countless answers.

You can make your own talking stick or magic wand using a stick from a tree or shrub. Carve various decorations into the bark (rings, spirals etc.) and add ribbons, feathers, beech etc.

Hazel sticks (like those of willow and elder) can most easily be carved with a pocket knife in spring, when the bark is full of juice. The bark can simply be peeled off so that the white wood becomes visible.

Individual trees symbolise certain qualities, which you may want to consider when making your talking stick:

 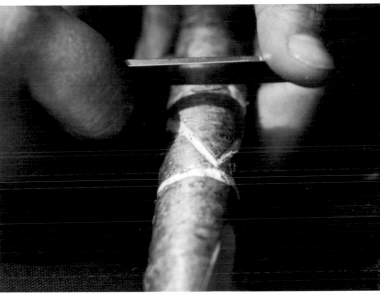

Experimenting with patterns for a talking stick or magic wand

Birch	Truth
Sycamore	Gentleness, loveliness
Hazel	Magic, prophetic
Ash	Protection
Oak	Strength, power
Fruit trees	Abundance, love
Walnut	Focusing of energies, starting projects

Summer

CRAFTS AND GAMES

Hazel rods can be widely used in games and crafts. Some ideas are given below.

Hazel beads

Saw twigs into slices of a desired thickness and make beads for a necklace. Hazel rods have soft pith that you can push out with a knitting needle, leaving a hole inside.

Hazel gnomes

You can turn a short length of hazel branch into an attractive little gnome. Simply paint on a face, beard and brightly coloured gnome hat and clothes. You can carve the end of your stick into a pointy hat, or sand it for a smoother finish.

Hazel gnomes hiding in the rushes

Diary sticks

Cut a 30 cm (1 ft) long hazel stick. Carve a new symbol for each day, leaving space for further days. Slowly, a kind of diary is created.

Finding inner peace

Cut at least a dozen hazel rods. Choose one of your favourite peaceful places outdoors and stick the rods in a circle into the ground to mark your chosen space. Sitting inside this circle, you can find peace and focus on your own thoughts.

Nine Man Morris

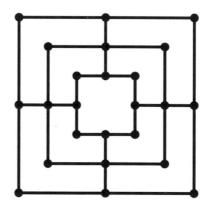

Nine Man Morris is a board game for two players that dates back to Roman times.

Mark the pattern of a Nine Man Morris board on a level piece of ground (e.g. a forest floor, gravel path or sand). Use 9 hazelnuts and 9 walnuts as men. The object of the game is to leave your opponent with less than 3 pieces or unable to make another move.

The game begins with an empty board, and players take turns to place their men on empty

82

spots, trying to form straight rows of 3 pieces along the board's lines (not diagonally). When a player makes a row of 3, it's called a 'mill', and he may remove one of his opponent's pieces from the board; removed pieces may not be placed again. Players must remove any other pieces first before removing a piece from a formed mill. Once all 18 pieces have been used, players take turns moving.

To move, a player slides one of his pieces along a board line to an empty adjacent spot. If he cannot move, he has lost the game. As in the placement stage, each time a player makes a new 'mill' he may remove one of his opponent's pieces, avoiding removing pieces in mills if at all possible. Any player with only 2 pieces remaining or who is unable to move loses the game.

LUCK AND PROTECTION

Protective charm

In the past, people had various rituals to protect their homes from harmful spirits. It was also essential to try and bring the protection of Mother Earth into the house, so people maintained a close relationship with nature. The Celts thought of some trees as especially holy and magical: hazel, apple, birch, oak, willow, holly and alder.

To make a protective charm, cut lengths of stick (up to around 10 cm, 4 in long) from at least five of these holy trees. Tie the bits of wood loosely together and hang them somewhere visible in the house. When fastening the lucky charm you can say the following words: 'Holy trees from times gone by, protect and guard my home.'

Nuts as bringers of luck and fertility

The nut is a symbol of fertility, wisdom and long life. The hazelnut was also thought of as an aphrodisiac. The hazel bush was even called the 'tree of temptation'. As regards fertility – which meant both being blessed with many children and a good harvest – a few customs involving nuts are still remembered: at weddings, nuts were thrown to the guests as good luck charms. The bride and bridegroom were supposed to eat lots of nuts so they would have many children, and they said that in years with plentiful nut harvests more children were born. On certain days, farmers gave three nuts to their cows to increase their fertility. Yet the nut was also a symbol of creative, productive ideas and for luck in general.

Good-luck nut charms

You can wish somebody good luck by giving them nuts wrapped in a piece of natural fabric or a leaf, tied with a ribbon or string. Or you could drill holes in nutshells and string them together to make a charm. There are many possibilities.

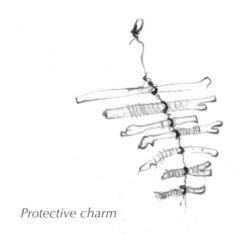

Protective charm

83

Autumn

THE NUT KITCHEN

Hazelnuts are ripe from the end of September onwards and can then be harvested. If we delay, the squirrels, dormice and mice will collect all the hazelnuts and walnuts as winter stores!

Hazelnuts are very versatile in the kitchen. They are tasty, rich in oil and protein and contain a lot of vitamin B6, which is an ideal food for building up and strengthening the nervous system: hazelnuts keep the mind healthy, they increase concentration and alleviate irritability. So, nuts are a popular snack with pupils and students. In cookery, nuts can be used in a variety of ways.

It is a common tradition in many cultures to celebrate the change of seasons with festivals, and autumn was the time of harvest festivals. People gave thanks for a bountiful harvest and asked for renewed fertility in the year to come. Therefore, at the beginning of autumn we can enjoy a nut festival. The following recipes are simple and well suited to this season.

Nut bread
500 g (1 lb) wholemeal flour
20 g (3/4 oz) yeast
1 teaspoon sea salt
300–350 ml (1 1/4 –1 1/2 cups) water
150 g (5 oz) walnuts and hazelnuts, mixed

Put the flour into a mixing bowl and make a well in the centre. Mix the yeast with a little lukewarm water and pour into the well. Add the remainder of the water, the salt and nuts.

Knead everything into a dough and shape into a loaf. Cover and leave to rise in a warm place until doubled in size.

Bake in a preheated oven at 220°C (430°F) for 40–50 minutes.

Serve with nut butter: mix together ground hazelnuts and butter.
(From Ingrid Schindler, *Die Nussküche*)

Nut Spaetzle (noodles)
200 g (7 oz) flour
30 g (1 oz) ground hazelnuts
100 ml (1/2 cup) water
1 teaspoon salt
2 eggs
1 tablespoon hazelnut oil

Mix all the ingredients into a soft dough until bubbly. Cut into 'Spaetzle' (thin noodles) and boil portion by portion in salty water. Lift out the Spaetzle and rinse with running cold water. Before serving, heat up in butter and add nutmeg and pepper.

Nut marzipan
100g (3 1/2 oz) finely ground hazelnuts
1 tablespoon creamy honey

Mix the ground hazelnuts with the honey. Knead by hand until the marzipan has a firm consistency. Refrigerate for one day before cutting out shapes. Add a few drops of beetroot juice to make pink marzipan.

Hazelnut soup

100 g (3 1/2 oz) ground hazelnuts
2 tablespoons butter
1 onion, finely chopped
1 litre (1 quart) vegetable stock
Salt and pepper
Parsley, chopped

Briefly dry roast the ground hazelnuts in a pan, then add the butter and onion. Add the vegetable stock and seasoning. Let the soup simmer for 15 minutes, and finally sprinkle with parsley.

Hazelnut milk

Boil up crushed hazelnuts in milk. This is helpful for persistent coughs.

Homemade dinner collected in nature tastes great

Winter

KEY SKILL: REFLECTION

The hazel is cleansing and purifying for body, soul and spirit and it generally has a calming effect. The hazel bush radiates a healthy lightness and looks youthful and happy. It's supposed to help in the attainment of wisdom. The Celtic people associated the hazel with knowledge. Roman mythology describes it as a symbol of peace and highlights it's mediating and balancing characteristics, which are essential for true dialogue and diplomacy. This in turn will enable us to understand ourselves and others.

Philosophy

Philosophy reflects on life, the meaning of things and the universe. Philosophy helps to develop the wisdom inherent within us, to ponder and find answers to essential questions. Why is the wisdom and 'seed' of a whole tree hidden in a small nut? Why do trees live longer than people? Why are the leaves shed in autumn?

Reflecting upon our own point of view and that of others leads to improved relationships. Only then will people be able to live peacefully together and treat the environment and nature in a compassionate way. Reflective, joyful, creative thinking and consideration will lead to practical answers, taking into account all different points of view.

Dilemma roleplays

To encourage the ability to reflect, we can make up 'dilemma stories'. A dilemma occurs when seemingly irreconcilable values come into conflict and it seems impossible to make a decision. First, the dilemma is presented, the respective points of view are outlined and various arguments are made transparent. Then everyone expresses their thoughts about what has been said. This is not about finding better arguments or about dominating the discussion. The aim is rather to create the space for a real dialogue, developing individual arguments so they can turn into decisions for the whole group. The process is about mutual understanding, being responsible for ourselves and the group, and ultimately being fair. It is often not possible to reach a decision about the actual dilemma.

The leader of the discussion should give suggestions, chair the discussion between individual arguments, and open up new avenues for mutual understanding. Specific questions formulated by members of the group are most helpful. The discussion can start with a story, which sets the scene. For the actual conversation, talking sticks are very helpful (see p.80).

Roleplay example

The four large hazel bushes that grow in front of the Mayor's house are going to be cut down. It is the only building site available for a new, urgently needed school building. But the hazel trees are well-loved and central to village life. Children love climbing the hazel bushes and in the afternoons older people often sit in their shade. However, the town councillors sometimes get annoyed about the noise and constant commotion outside.

Distribute the various roles: councillors, grandmother, teacher, father, girl, gardener who takes care of the green spaces in the village. Each group member should take on their role and attempt to explain their point of view and to contribute to the decision.

Offering our point of view and reflecting on other people's opinions.
Whoever holds the talking stick takes their turn to speak.

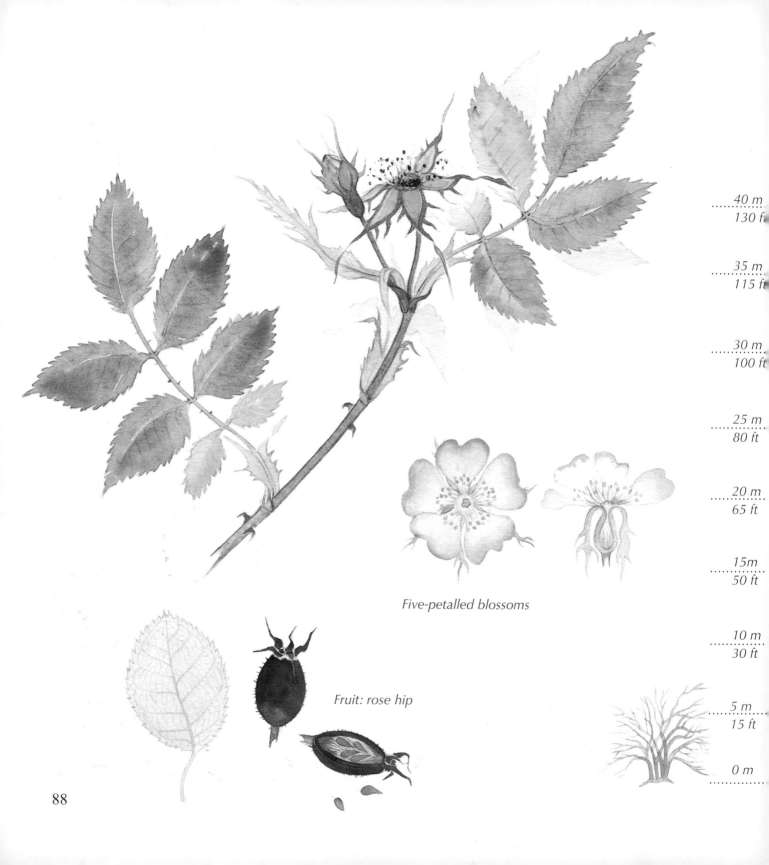

Five-petalled blossoms

Fruit: rose hip

40 m
130 ft

35 m
115 ft

30 m
100 ft

25 m
80 ft

20 m
65 ft

15m
50 ft

10 m
30 ft

5 m
15 ft

0 m

8. Hedge Rose – Tree of Scents

HABITAT AND CHARACTERISTICS

The hedge rose, which is also called dog rose or sweet briar, likes to grow in sunny places beside footpaths, along the margins of woodlands and in meadows, or it is used as hedging around houses and fields. It's a very prickly though attractive shrub without any particular demands on the soil it grows in. The hedge rose has arching stems and may grow a few metres high. In early summer the bush is adorned with sweet-smelling, pale pink flowers which turn into red 'false' fruits, commonly called rose hips, in autumn. Birds love to eat the rose hips and thus the seeds are spread. Rose trees may live for several hundred years.

Over the centuries the various original rose species have been used to create manifold different varieties by crossing and grafting. Today about 7000 different varieties are known the world over. The celebrated sisters of the hedge rose are grown in all cultures and gardens and they are held in high esteem everywhere. The rose is a powerful symbol in many stories.

ALL SORTS OF USES

Traditionally the flowers of the dog rose were used as a natural remedy and food.

An infusion of its petals, together with sage leaves, was recommended as a gargle to treat sore throats. The petals were thought to be a good cure for diarrhoea. Prepared as mouthwash, blossom tincture of hedge rose helped to heal bleeding gums. Taken inwardly, the tincture strengthens both the heart and nerves. Dried and powdered rose petals were used in powder form to treat children's wounds. Rose-bud tea was thought to be an effective haemostatic and antispasmodic.

In monasteries, rose petals were added to sweets and fish dishes. Even today, people use the petals to flavour cakes, make rose sugar, rose jam, rose juice, or rose syrup.

Spring

ART IN NATURE

There are hardly any places left in nature that are untouched by man. People shape, dominate and structure their natural surroundings. It's attractive to create art in and with nature – at the same time this is a subtle way of dealing with the issue of nature being dominated by man. The aim is to leave traces consisting solely of natural materials. Nothing gets destroyed and yet it will become obvious that people spent time at that particular place. Through hanging our works of art in a tree, or laying them somewhere, natural art is given back to nature again, leaving our trace.

Use rose blossoms and other flowers, pieces of sticks, leaves, feathers, snail shells, fir cones or stones to create circles, tie rings with them or build small towers.

Natural mandalas

Mandalas are sacred circles known in many cultures. They symbolise both the eternal cycle of life and the path to the centre of our inner being. Laying a mandala and observing it has a centering and calming effect.

Use a variety of natural materials to create different kinds of circles. Blossoms and rose leaves, rose hips and other natural materials are well suited to laying mandalas.

You can work from the periphery to the centre or the other way round. You can also divide the design of various sections of the circle between individual group members.

Spot the difference game

You can make a fun game out of spotting the difference between objects that belong in their surroundings and others that we have placed there. Find a natural space outside, and move items around or add items that obviously don't belong to the original natural scene: put an empty snail shell onto a branch, make a stone pile, lay spruce cones around a tree in a regular pattern, fasten an evergreen twig to a deciduous tree etc.

Ask your group if they can tell what has always been there and what was changed by human hands. Who will find out how many things were changed?

Nature ring

Make a plait from the flexible branches of willow, hazel or clematis. Tie a selection of natural objects to it and hang up somewhere as decoration. This is a particularly effective way of bringing nature into an urban setting.

Leaf amulet

Punch three holes into a small piece of leather. Thread a leather thong or string through one of the holes. Put leaves of hedge rose or of other trees into the other two holes. Perhaps such amulets can protect us and bring us luck.

Human traces left in nature

Making a leaf amulet

Mandalas laid with blossoms, leaves and twigs

Summer

KEY SKILL: WELL-BEING

Whether a person feels good or not depends on both inner and outer factors. Radiating health, positive thinking and energy are seen as signs of well-being. Of all plants it is the rose that invites us most to relax. It has been known for centuries that roses (hedge roses as well as cultivated roses) are beneficial for body and soul. Roses have a strengthening and cooling effect. Scents in general and particularly the rose scent induce relaxation and a sense of well-being.

In numerous plant books the rose is called the queen of plants. She symbolises beauty, love and innocence. She is the subject of songs and has been praised in many a poem. Traditionally, lovers give each other an uneven amount of roses as a sign of deep affection. Well-to-do people loved to bathe in rose water. In ancient Rome roses were extremely popular: petals were strewn on the ground to make carpets for celebrations and victors were showered with them.

Various cosmetic or culinary products may influence our physical and psychological well-being in a positive way.

HOME REMEDIES

Rose-petal tea
Rose petals or buds are delicious in herb tea mixtures.

Pour 1 litre (1 quart) of boiling water over 2 handfuls of fresh or 1 handful of dried rose petals. Infuse for 10 minutes and strain. Rose petals go well with mint, lemon balm, lime flowers and calendula.

Preparations made with rose petals stimulate our senses; they strengthen our heart and nerves and have a cooling effect. The petals can also be used as compresses for swollen eyelids.

Rose water for health and cooking
Steep rose petals in hot water for 1 hour. Strain and bottle. Keep unopened bottles refrigerated, use opened bottles within a week.

To treat headaches and fever, put rose-water compresses on the forehead or temples; these compresses also have a soothing effect on the circulatory and digestive system.

You can add rose water to various dishes: salad dressings, couscous and meat dishes and desserts. Supposedly rose water is also an aphrodisiac.

Rose vinegar
Briefly warm up some fruit vinegar and pour over a few rose petals. Use the extracted and strained rose vinegar for salad dressings. Thinned down with water it may also be taken as a gargle for sore throats.

Essential oil of rose
The essential oil is distilled from petals of scented roses. For obtaining one drop of essential oil, you will need approximately 30 rose blossoms. Rose oil has an important place in aromatherapy. The scent is calming and helps with anxiety and depression.

Homemade rose tea is especially tasty

Rose massage oil

Mix 20 ml (2/3 fl oz) of almond oil with 3–5 drops of essential oil of rose. Use to treat stress, exhaustion and constipation.

Face tonic

15 drops essential oil
30 ml (1 fl oz) cosmetic alcohol
50 ml (1 2/3 fl oz) rose water
25 ml (3/4–1 fl oz) orange blossom water

Dissolve the essential oil in the alcohol. Then mix all the ingredients together and keep in a glass bottle. Face tonics are refreshing and vitalising.

Rose bath

Bring to the boil 5 handfuls of rose petals in 1–2 litres (1–2 quarts) of water. Simmer at a low heat for 15 minutes, strain and then add to the bath water. Rose petals are ideal skincare and have a relaxing effect.

Rose balm

100 ml (1/2 cup) olive or almond oil
2 teaspoons lanolin
10 g (1/3 oz) beeswax
1 handful rose petals
3 ml (1/10 fl oz) rose tincture
15–20 drops essential oil of rose

Warm up the oil, lanolin and beeswax in a double boiler. Add the rose petals and let the mixture steep on a low heat, then strain. Add the rose tincture (pour cosmetic alcohol over some rose petals, infuse for 5 minutes, strain). Drip the essential oil into an ointment jar and pour the balm mixture into it. Let it cool down completely before closing the lid.

Applying rose balm – a treat for the skin

Autumn

ROSE HIPS – NATURAL REMEDY AND SWEET DELIGHT

In the olden times, traditional remedies were made from the leaves, blossoms, fruit and even the roots of hedge roses. Today only preparations from the fruits are common. Archaeological findings from the site of the lake-dwelling settlement at Lake Constance in Germany show that rose hips were used as far back as the Stone Age. Even nowadays, they are known for being healthy and nourishing and for their medicinal uses.

Rose hips are ready to be harvested after the bush has lost most of its leaves in late autumn. Inside the 'false' fruits there are small seeds, which are the actual fruits. The rose hip is rich in minerals and contains various vitamins. Its vitamin C content is many times higher than that of citrus fruit.

Rose hips can be made into tea, jam, desserts, soups, liquor and even wine. Before processing, cut up the fruits and remove the seeds and hair (they cause itchiness!). The seeds of the rose hip were not thrown away by our ancestors but used as a remedy for dropsy (edema), rheumatism and sciatica.

Pre-winter vitamin therapy

In autumn, try eating one fresh rose hip mornings and evenings for three weeks. This will give you a vitamin boost, which can strengthen your immune system. Cut the picked rose hip in half and remove the seeds and hair.

Harvesting rose hips in autumn

Rose-hip tea

One handful of rose hips is enough for one cup of tea. Halve the rose hips, remove the seeds and put into cold water, which you then bring to the boil. Simmer for 10 minutes and let the tea steep for a further 15 minutes. Rose-hip tea is diuretic and blood-purifying. It strengthens the body's defences and helps with rheumatism and gout. You can also prepare a refreshing cold beverage from rose hips.

When dried, rose hips hardly contain any vitamin C, although many other ingredients are preserved.

Rose-hip jam

200 g (7 oz) rose-hip halves
100 g (3 1/2 oz) sugar

Wash the rose hips and cook on a low heat in a little water until soft. Blend the rose hips and the fluid to a purée using a mouli or sieve. Add the sugar and boil up the mixture for 2–3 minutes. Pour the rose-hip jam into jars.

Gnomes' soup

Gnomes know various magic dishes to stay well all through the winter. They revealed one of their recipes to us:

Remove the seeds and hair of fresh rose hips, wash them and purée in a food processor. Mix some water with white or red wine. Add sugar, lemon zest and the puréed rose hips and briefly bring to the boil. Mix the soup with freshly grated apple and breadcrumbs.

(From Eve Marie Heim, *Feld- Wald-und Wiesenkochbuch*)

Winter

MAGIC APPLES

The sting of the mossy rose gall wasp sometimes creates a growth in hedge roses. In some countries these galls are called rose apples or sleeping apples. A few centuries ago they were still sold as herbal remedies. They were meant to induce calm deep sleep and were placed under children's pillows. Sometimes they were also used to perform magic.

The gnome Laurin and his gnome friends live in a ruined castle high up on a rock. Humans hardly ever find their way up there. Everything is completely overgrown with thorny rose bushes and only the gnomes are able to move freely under those roses. Now and again a young boy tries to climb the crumbling tower to look for the treasure which is meant to be hidden there.

One winter, an especially brave and nimble boy managed to reach the top of the tower. But just as he was trying to lay his hands on the highest ledge, one of the walls of the tower collapsed. The gnomes got a big fright. But the worst thing was that their beloved rose bushes were buried under all the stones. For the rose bushes were their source of medicine and food, and they made a beautiful rose garden as well – with its lovely scents in summer and its glowing colours in autumn. They feared that their roses were lost forever. The following spring the rose garden remained bare and wizened. But the summer after that the rose bushes started to grow new shoots again.

To stop this happening again, Laurin and his friends thought of a plan. For generations the gnomes had made protective charm bags with herbs, wild fruit and sometimes a piece of wood. They wore these little bags around their necks or kept them hidden in a secret place. Ever since the tower collapsed, they have added rose petals and rose apples to the contents of these bags. The furry apples of the hedge rose had the power to attract humans and then they would magically make them fall fast asleep for a very long time. Now, when the gnomes saw a young lad coming up the hill, they would quickly take out their rose apples and petals from their bags and use the fragrance to entice the invader into a cave, where he fell asleep. When he awoke after many days, he was so hungry and thirsty that he hurried home. Since hedge roses do not only make humans feel sleepy but also forgetful, the secret of the gnomes has never been betrayed.

So if you come upon a thicket of roses, beware – perhaps Laurin and his friends are dwelling in there.

MAKING POT-POURRI

Just like many of the other tree products, the blossoms and buds of the hedge rose (of course also those of the cultivated rose) can be collected in summer and dried in a shady place. In winter, mix the dried petals with various other dried plant materials such as fir needles, elderflower blossoms, hazel bark, rose hips and juniper twigs to create fragrant pot-pourris. You can put your pot-pourri into homemade bags to make lovely Christmas gifts.

For a more intense fragrance, add a few drops of essential oil of rose or fir to the mixture as you place it in a bowl for display.

The sting of the mossy rose gall wasp produces round galls, known as rose apples

9. Elder – Tree of Good Luck

HABITAT AND CHARACTERISTICS

Apart from the far north, the elder is found throughout the world. It flourishes in hedges and on the edge of woodland. It often takes root near houses as it loves being close to people. The stems of the elder can easily be hollowed out and used to make whistles.

ALL SORTS OF USES

In popular tradition the elder is of great importance as a 'medicine chest' and magic plant. Not only flowers and berries but also the bark, leaves and roots were used. Elder was used to treat bruises and sprains, and the leaves were cooked in lard and made into ointment. The bark was used as a strong laxative.

People also entrusted the elder tree with their treasures. If a family had to suddenly leave their home, they would bury their most precious things under the elder tree. Upon returning, even after many years, they knew exactly where to find their treasures.

Elderberries can be used to dye food, craft work and cosmetic products.

Elderflowers can be used to flavour many foods and drinks, particularly beverages such as cordial and wine.

In order to get rid of voles or field mice, elder leaves are stuffed into their holes and tunnels or a piece of elder wood is put into the ground nearby. The mice cannot stand the smell of the wood and wander off.

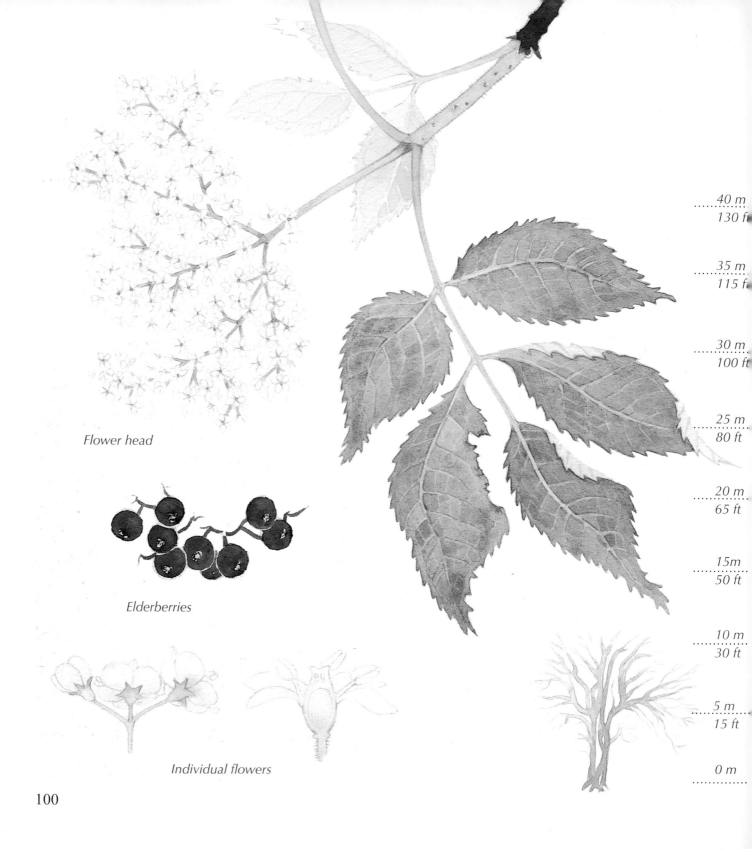

Flower head

Elderberries

Individual flowers

40 m
130 ft

35 m
115 ft

30 m
100 ft

25 m
80 ft

20 m
65 ft

15m
50 ft

10 m
30 ft

5 m
15 ft

0 m

Spring

ELDERFLOWER RECIPES

The elder is extremely versatile in the kitchen whilst also being a popular medicinal plant. From May through to July the tree is full of flowers – white, sweet smelling blooms! You can pick the flower heads and use them straight away or, alternatively, dry them in a warm, shady place.

Elderflower tea

Pour 1 cup of boiling water onto 1 head of elderflower and leave to infuse for 5 minutes.

This tea is used to treat fevers, influenza, colds and catarrhal inflammations. It also has a calming effect, strengthens the immune system and is used to treat rheumatism, gout, infections and to cleanse skin. In traditional medicine elderflower tea applied as a poultice relieves headaches, earaches and toothaches. You can also simply drink it to enjoy its delicate taste!

Elderflower milk

Boil up 1–2 flower heads in 1 cup of milk, infuse and strain. Add vanilla or cinnamon according to taste and sweeten with honey.

Elderflower syrup

20 elderflower heads
1/2 litre (1/2 quart) water
500 g (1 lb) sugar
1 lemon

Mix together the water, sugar and the sliced lemon, bring to the boil and pour onto the blossoms. Cover the container and let the mixture steep for three days. Strain and fill well-cleaned bottles up to the brim. The unopened bottles will keep up to half a year in the fridge.

Granny's elderflower lemonade

6 litres (6 quarts) water
750 g (1 2/3 lb) sugar
12 elderflower heads
2 lemons, sliced
100 ml (1/2 cup) vinegar

Put all the ingredients into a stoneware pot or a glass bowl, cover with a cloth and place outdoors. After approximately 3–5 days the fermentation process starts. You can also bottle the lemonade and keep it in the fridge for a short while. Take care when opening the bottles!

Elderflower pancakes

At the time of the summer solstice people used to eat elder blossoms cooked in a pancake batter. A delicacy loved by nearly everyone!

An elderflower sandwich

Spread a slice of bread with butter and garnish with elderflowers. This is unusual but delicious!

Trying out simple cooking and medicinal recipes

Summer

KEY SKILL: RELIABILITY, CONNECTION WITH THE EARTH

The elder tree is often placed by the house or barn as a protective spirit. People used to treat it with respect – women curtsied when passing by and men lifted their hats. In return for their appreciation people believed that the tree gave health and good luck to them, their homes and farms. Nobody dared to fell an elder without asking its forgiveness.

The magic powers of the elder were supposed to drive away diseases. The tree was thought to attract evil forces and conduct them into the ground. That is also the reason why people entrusted it with their precious belongings.

Elder good-luck amulet
With a hand drill or a thin knitting needle, push out the pith of small sections of an elder stem. Thread the elder rings together with wooden beads and other natural objects onto a string or leather thong.

An elder charm is believed to bring good luck, to help us stay connected to the earth and to promote equanimity.

Grounding and reliability
In school reports and employment references reliability is mentioned over and over again. This virtue is highly esteemed in our society. When making agreements and coming to decisions we need to be able to rely on ourselves and others.

If people are unreliable, they are no longer fully connected with themselves nor with the world around them. When sufficiently connected to the natural world we also become calm and trusting.

The elder encourages reliability and has a calming and soothing effect. It facilitates a closeness to the earth and a sense of being 'grounded'.

The elder tree and earth spirits

The elder was thought to be the entrance gate to the realm of Mother Earth or 'Mother Holle'. This goddess dwelling beneath the elder was believed to look after the souls of dead animals and people. She led them into the underworld and then released them to begin a new cycle of life. Mother Earth was also the queen of gnomes and elves, and the elder grew at the threshold to the kingdom of the gnomes.

In northern countries they say that on the night of the summer solstice the elf king passes by, and whoever sits under the elder bush can observe this scene. And if you sleep under the elder, you are supposed to be able to feel the presence of the earth spirits, the gnomes, goblins and dwarves. The overhanging branches form a kind of roof and invite us to spend some time under it on warm days. Who knows what we will see in a quiet moment? Maybe we would like to drink some elderflower tea or elderflower milk while we're there.

Elder incense

In some magical rituals the elder is used as an incense plant. To get in contact with the realm of the earth and its spirits, you can use dried elder wood, pith, bark, flowers and even the roots for making incense (see p.73).

It's easy to make amulets from bits of elder stem. Hollow out the stem, decide on an order and string together your elder and decorations

104

Autumn

ELDERBERRY RECIPES

Elderberries ripen in September and October. Watch out: unripe berries that are still green on the inside are mildly poisonous! The berries should only be eaten when cooked. They provide us with vitamins and minerals. You can also dry them for storage.

Elderberries (just like the blossoms) help us to cope with the rigours of cold weather in winter.

Elderberry jam

Use a fork to remove the berries from the stalks. Simmer approximately 200 g (7 oz) of berries in a little water until soft, then pass them through a sieve or a mouli. Slice two apples, cook and purée.

Mix equal parts of the puréed elderberries and apples and then add half the weight of the fruit in sugar and the corresponding amount of gelling agent. Boil the mixture and pour into jars while still hot. You can use the same recipe to make jam without apples as well.

Elderberry juice

Strip the berries off the stalks, just cover with water and simmer until soft. Pass them through a sieve or a mouli. Add the same weight in sugar and boil the berry juice down to a syrup consistency. Bottle and close the lids straight away.

Elderberry juice relieves colds and other respiratory illnesses such as angina, coughs and sore throats. The juice is also effective in cleansing the blood and bowels. It's rich in vitamins, quenches the thirst and can also be drunk hot.

Mulled elderberry punch

1/2 litre (1/2 quart) elderberry juice (pressed from the berries)
1–2 cloves
1 cinnamon stick
A small amount of orange or lemon juice
1 tablespoon honey

Heat up the elderberry juice with the cloves and cinnamon. Strain the spices. Add orange or lemon juice and honey. Serve hot.

Elderberry soup

This sweet elderberry soup is a source of energy during the cold season.

Put ripe elderberries into a pot and cover well with water, cook and strain. Flavour with sugar, cinnamon and lemon zest and thicken with a little flour. Before serving, add a bit of cream and sprinkle fried bread cubes over it.

Winter

ELDER MUSIC

The elder has always had great significance for human beings. It is the focus of stories, songs and poems. This tree is also called the 'tree of music' because the stems were often bored with holes and fashioned into flutes for making music.

Homemade elderberry products taste best on cold days in autumn and winter

The Elder Tree Song

Tree, you lovely tree.
You grow big and sturdy.
Every year a little bit,
grow, you lovely tree!

Tree, you tree of spring,
stretch your branches further,
sprout green leaves and give us shade,
grow, you lovely tree!

Tree, you summer tree,
show us all your blossoms,
fragrant scent so sweet and fine,
bloom, you lovely tree.

Tree of harvest time,
carry ripened fruit,
new life born of hidden seeds,
ripen, lovely tree!

Tree, you winter tree,
through the branches bare
may we see the sky so clear,
wait, you lovely tree.

(Lyrics translated from a German song by Barbara Cratzius; music: Ludger Edelkötte)

Actions and props for The Elder Tree Song

In preparation for the activity, paint symbolic leaves, flowers and fruit onto white card and cut them out. You could even try these natural dyes as paints:

Green paint for the leaves: made from the leaves of willow, birch, stinging nettle or dandelion

Cream or yellow paint for the flowers: made from the petals of elderflowers or dandelion heads

Red paint for the fruit: made from elderberries or beetroot

Chop up the collected leaves, add water, bring to the boil and simmer until the colour is a strong hue, then strain. Cook the fruit, squash with a fork and strain. Pour the fluids into glass jars and label them. These water-based paints keep in the fridge for a few days.

The group forms a circle. Each child represents a tree. They perform movements according to the content of each verse, holding up the various symbols, swaying to and fro etc.

1st verse: The human trees squat and slowly grow

2nd verse: The human trees slowly wake. They wave their green paper leaves.

3rd verse: The human trees stretch themselves. They move their white blossoms about.

4th verse: The human trees hold their red fruit in their hands and sway.

5th verse: The human trees stand motionless with empty hands and spread fingers.

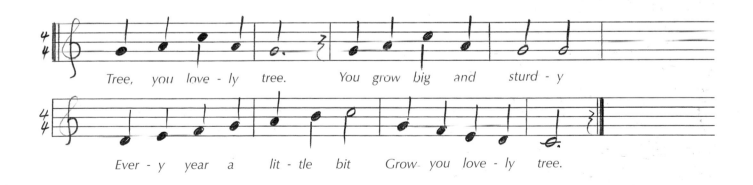

Tree, you love - ly tree. You grow big and sturd - y

Ever - y year a lit - tle bit Grow you love - ly tree.

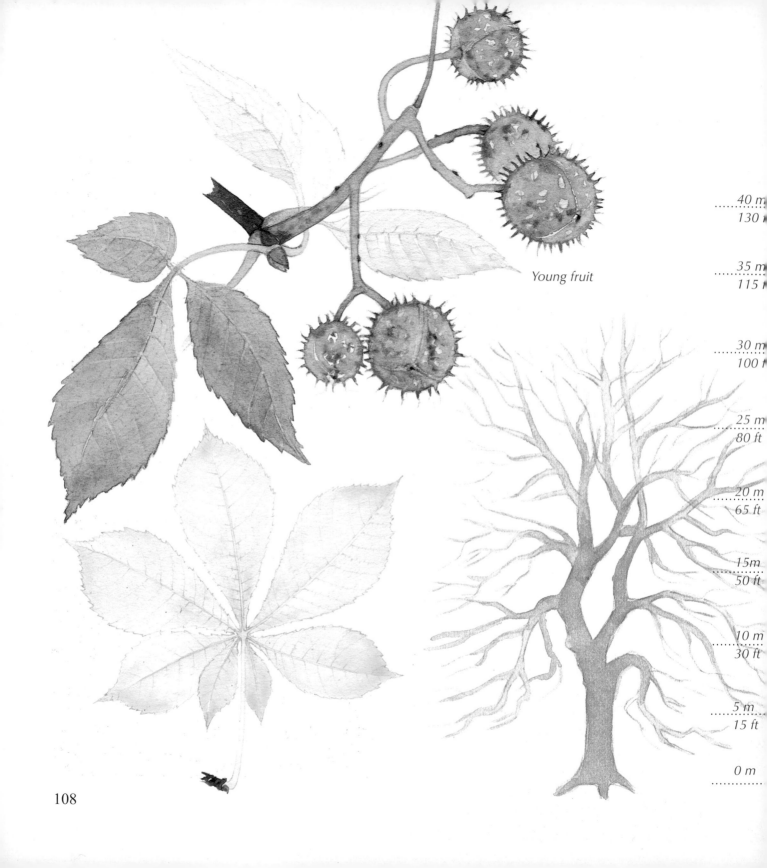

Young fruit

40 m
130 f

35 m
115 f

30 m
100 f

25 m
80 ft

20 m
65 ft

15m
50 ft

10 m
30 ft

5 m
15 ft

0 m

108

10. Horse Chestnut – Sociable Tree

HABITAT AND CHARACTERISTICS

The chestnut – also commonly known as horse chestnut – was introduced to Central Europe from the Balkans in the 16th century. This tree can attain a height of 30 m (almost 100 feet). Its buds are very sticky and the leaves are made up of 5–7 conspicuous finger-like leaflets. The huge 'candles' of flowers resembling orchids bloom in May and June. When summer has come to an end, glossy mahogany-coloured seeds emerge from the prickly round green fruits.

North of the Alps the sweet chestnut is much less common than the horse chestnut; it grows mostly in Mediterranean regions. These trees are not related to each other, so their leaves and flowers differ considerably, but their fruits are quite similar.

ALL SORTS OF USES

The horse chestnut is still well known today as a medicinal plant. It's one of the most important remedies for treating vein diseases and is applied to relieve varicose veins, venous congestions and inflammations. It's also recommended for treating damaged invertebral discs, bruises and sports injuries. Since aescin, an active constituent of the horse chestnut, absorbs ultra-violet rays, it is used in sun protection products.

For medicinal purposes, collect the flowers (May, June), leaves, fruits (September to October, when the peel is brown) and the bark. The leaves and flowers are infused. A decoction can be prepared from the bark. Tea made from the blossoms is an expectorant for coughs and the flower tincture is used as liniment in rheumatism.

Horse chestnut used to be part of snuff mixtures and it was also sniffed to prevent colds.

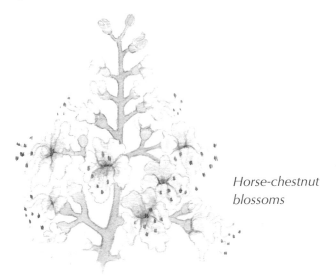

Horse-chestnut blossoms

109

The horse chestnut is a tree of well-being, plenty and riches. It gives generous shade in summer

Spring

TREE SONG

(Song by Monika Baur)

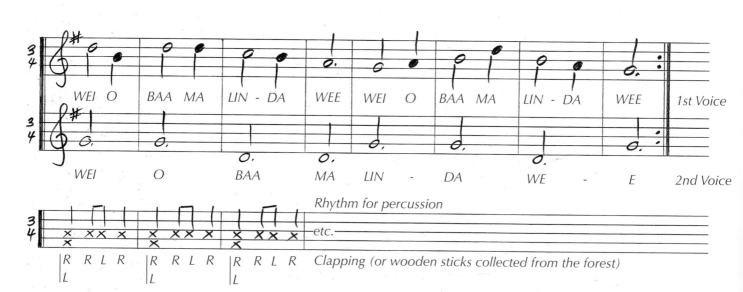

Rhythm sticks

The tree song is accompanied with wooden rhythm sticks. Everyone looks for two sturdy wooden sticks. Children form a circle and the leader suggests a rhythm. One after the other, each child copies it. You can hear the rhythm going round the circle. Then you can change the rhythm, its complexity, volume and tempo. To finish, try to construct a sculpture in the middle of the circle using the sticks.

Children accompany the tree song with rhythm sticks

Summer

KEY SKILL: TEAM WORK

The horse chestnut does not like being on its own. It loves the company of its own kind and also of people. With its imposing flowers and leaves it seems to wish to attract attention. Horse chestnut trees are often found in garden restaurants, parks, gardens and alleyways as well as on village greens, their dense foliage providing a lot of welcome shade. The atmosphere is quite special under a chestnut tree, which makes it a popular place for social gatherings.

Living and working together demands a whole variety of qualities that are vital for successful human relationships. The ability to work in a team includes: co-operation, being prepared to give your consent, loyalty, tolerance, flexibility, consideration, respect, being able to listen and to state your own opinion, taking on responsibility for the group, being able to admit weak points and mistakes, recognising and making use of differing viewpoints.

Using all your senses

Horse chestnut trees help us to calm down and they support self-reflection. It's good to spend a few silent minutes with the chestnut tree, and use all your senses to be completely with the tree. Do you hear the leaves rustle? Do you notice the buds, flowers and leaves in all their beauty? Are you aware of the tree's scent? Can you lie under the roof of leaves and marvel at the green sky as the sun sends its bright rays through leaves that are happily waving at us? You are resting and at one with the tree.

Organising a tree festival

Festivals promote community spirit, joy and happiness. They form a contrast to our daily lives. We experience festivals with all our senses: hearing, seeing, touching, smelling and tasting.

A tree festival can be organised by a team whose members decide on the programme, send out invitations, plan what equipment is needed and share out the tasks.

Put on a tree bar and buffet, with elderflower syrup, lime-blossom tea, lime-blossom sandwiches, nut cupcakes, apple cake, nut bread, elderberry jam etc.
Make decorations using various parts of trees.
Play music on homemade instruments: wooden rhythm sticks (see p.111), rattles, xylophones, string instruments and even whistles (see p.106).

Torches

In the past, before electricity was available, people lit up the darkness with homemade torches. A special atmosphere is created at the tree festival when these torches are burning.

Lay cotton rags that have been dipped into melted wax around the top of a stick, making sure the stick is long enough to be easily held. Wind several layers of rags on top of each other and fasten them.

Tree festival with music, torches and food collected in nature

114

Autumn

MEDICINAL, TASTY AND CLEANSING FRUITS

In autumn, dozens of shiny mahogany-coloured chestnuts (conkers) are waiting to be picked up by children, who love to play with them and make various figures and animals from them. The following uses are less well known.

Pocket chestnut

Even nowadays, you can sometimes hear the recommendation that carrying a chestnut prevents rheumatism and gout. You can keep it in a little bag, in your trouser pocket or attach it as a pendant to a small chain around your neck. This could be especially helpful for longer bicycle tours and horse-riding excursions to avoid painful chafing.

Carrying a chestnut in your pocket is also supposed to help let go of stubbornness and fixed ideas.

Horse chestnuts for animals

As the popular name of the chestnut already indicates, its fruit are often given to horses. Many wild animals also love bitter horse chestnuts. Now and again you can add chopped-up chestnuts to food for small pets for extra strength.

Chestnuts for gourmets

The fruits of the horse chestnut are too bitter for human tastebuds, yet this can easily be remedied. To de-bitter chestnuts, soak them in a mixture of milk and water overnight. Then strain the fluid and boil the chestnuts in fresh water. Repeat this procedure until the fruit no longer tastes bitter.

Now the chestnuts may be dried or roasted and then ground. Flour that has been de-bittered in this way can be used as starch and added to biscuits and soups.

Horse-chestnut skin gel

3 teaspoons horse chestnut tincture (see below)
10 drops essential oil of lavender
80 ml (2 3/4 fl oz) rose tea
1 level tablespoon guar gum (gelling agent)

Steep chopped horse chestnuts in alcohol for three weeks, then strain. Dissolve the essential oil in this tincture. Add the cooled rose tea and the guar gum. Close the container and shake well. This refreshing liniment gel is strengthening and has a nurturing, smoothing effect on the skin. It firms the connective tissue and invigorates tired feet and legs. Medicinally, it can be used to treat varicose veins and other painful vein conditions.

Washing agent

Chestnuts contain a saponin, and produce a soap-like foam when mixed with water. The flour made from ground chestnuts may be used to wash rough and cracked hands.

For a bath, chop up six handfuls of chestnuts, soak in water overnight, briefly bring to the boil, strain and add the fluid to the bath water. Froth will form on the water. A chestnut bath helps with circulation disorders, rheumatism and gout.

Chestnuts also used to be the base of a kind of glue used for book binding and wall papering. It was supposed to repel insects and protect from dampness.

Winter

TREE GAMES

We can play tree-related games at any time of the year.

Goblins and Trolls

In this fun game, teams of children pretend to be goblins and trolls. The goblins want to raid the store of chestnuts belonging to the trolls, but the trolls defend themselves.

Mark a playing field approximately 30 m (100 ft) long in a wood, at the edge of a forest or in a park. Mark a starting line. Deposit the chestnuts at the other end of the playing field. The trolls, who are each equipped with a soft ball, hide themselves behind trees (at least 10 m, 33 ft from the starting line).

The game begins. The goblins try to get the chestnuts and take them to their cave behind the starting line. The trolls attempt to hit the goblins with the balls. They are only allowed to throw, not to run and throw. Whoever is hit by a ball is eliminated from the game. Every chestnut taken is one point. Later the parts are swapped.

Chestnut Mice

With a needle, make holes through a few chestnuts, thread strings through them and fasten them securely. The game is played with these little 'mice' as figures. Put the mice onto a flat surface, such as a tree stump. The 'tree owl', equipped with a plastic mug and a dice, tries to catch the mice. If a 2 or a 4 is thrown, the tree owl can try

to catch a mouse with the mug. The mice may be pulled back by their tails as soon as the owl starts to hunt. Whoever is caught by the owl becomes the owl next. If more than one mouse is caught, they roll the dice and the player with the highest score becomes the owl. If you pull back your mouse too early, you have to do a forfeit or lose a point, depending on the agreed rules.

Rooted Trees

Use branches to mark a playing field. One player tries to catch the others. If they are touched by the catcher, they turn into trees and remain standing as if rooted to the ground. The 'trees' may also try to catch others by touching them as they run by. The game is finished when there are only rooted trees and the catcher left on the playing field.

Throwing games

You can invent numerous throwing games and games of skill using chestnuts, acorns or fir cones: for example, standing at a marked line, who can throw the highest number of chestnuts into a hollow tree trunk? How often will you manage to hit a certain branch?

Elves and Gnomes

In a level park or a piece of woodland with little undergrowth, mark 3–5 trees (for 10–12 players) with cloths or branches.

Two gnomes (who are recognisable by an item of clothing, such as a red hat) attempt to catch the elves. The safe spots for the elves are the marked trees. However, only one elf is allowed per tree. If a new elf comes along, the elf who was there already has to leave. A caught (touched) elf turns into a gnome as well – and is given a hat to wear. The game finishes when no more elves can be caught.

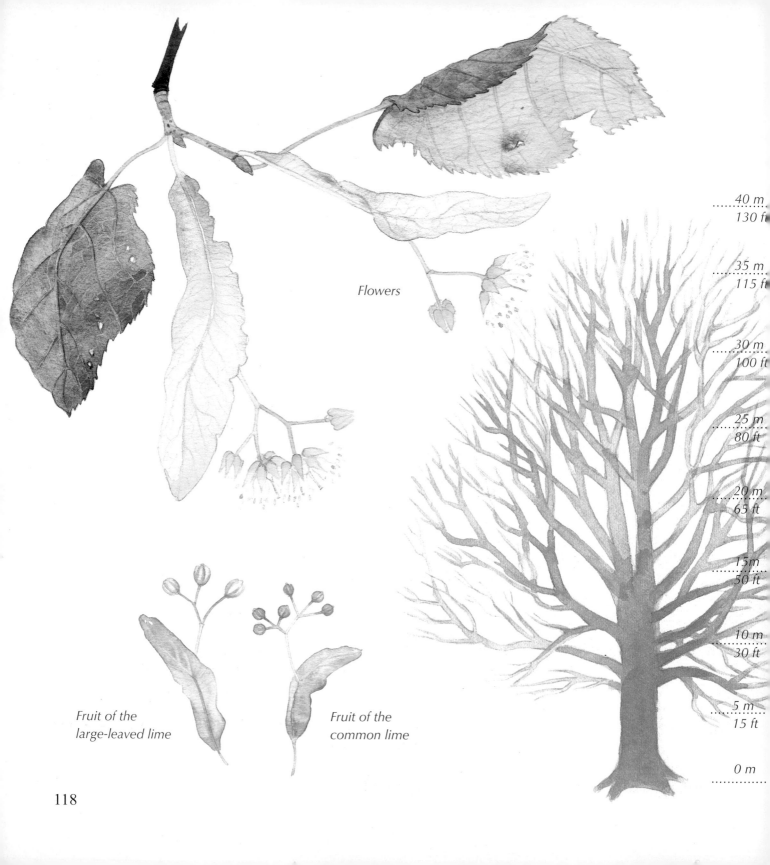

Flowers

Fruit of the
large-leaved lime

Fruit of the
common lime

40 m
130 ft

35 m
115 ft

30 m
100 ft

25 m
80 ft

20 m
65 ft

15m
50 ft

10 m
30 ft

5 m
15 ft

0 m

118

11. Lime (Linden) — Tree of Communication

HABITAT AND CHARACTERISTICS

The lime (linden) is common throughout the northern hemisphere. It is found in altitudes of up to 1000 m (^{2}/3 mile) and can reach an age of 1000 years. Limes grow in mixed forests, along the margins of woods, in hedges, and they are planted as individual trees in parks, avenues and around houses. Over the course of time the trunk of the tree often becomes rotten inside and newly formed aerial roots inside the trunk take over the nourishing function. The lime tree is very sensitive to pollution, which is why today many of them are sickly or are struggling to survive in cities. Botanists make the distinction between the large-leaved lime (*Tilia platyphyllos*) and the common lime (*Tilia europaea*). The large-leaved lime flowers some weeks before the common lime. Both varieties are used in the same way.

ALL SORTS OF USES

Lime-tree products are useful in cookery, crafts and medicine. In the past, bast fibres from the bark were made into paper, mats and even clothes. Later on, people made ropes and baskets from the lime's bast. To do this, the soft inner layer of the bark is peeled off, tied into bunches and soaked in water. The bast comes off and can then be dried and processed.

Beside the Village Fountain

Beside the village fountain,
There stands a linden tree.
How often in her shadow
Sweet dreams have come to me!
Upon her bark, there, carving,
Designs of love I made.
Both happiness and sorrow,
Would draw me to her shade,
Would draw me to her shade.

Alas! I had to wander,
Before the dawn's first light.
I passed her in the darkness,
Which hid her from my sight.
Her branches rustled gently,
As if she spoke to me,
'Come here, beloved companion!
Here, peace shall comfort thee,
Here, peace shall comfort thee.'

The cruel winds were blowing
Cold rain into my face.
My anguished heart was crying,
While I increased my pace.
Though many miles, now, distant from
That dear old linden tree,
My mind still hears her promise:
'Here, peace you'll find with me!
Here, peace you'll find with me!'

(Lyrics by Wilhelm Müller, set to music by Franz Schubert)

Spring

THE TREE OF THE PEOPLE

The lime is a tree of the people and was often planted in the middle of a village or in front of a house. It was also much valued near people's homes because it was supposed to give protection from lightning and evil spirits. Lime trees were also thought to be helpful in predicting the future. Even nowadays, you can often find a solitary lime tree in front of a church, at a well or in a yard.

Underneath its green roof, which is made up of many hundreds of heart-shaped leaves, people celebrated their festivals, with dancing, singing, storytelling, and so on. The branches of 'dancing limes' were trained in such a way that a dance floor could be built on top of them. Lime trees would probably be able to tell many a love story – love and the lime tree have always belonged together.

Lime trees were considered to be trees of destiny and as such they were often planted to commemorate certain events. Many of the solitary limes standing on hills in Germany were planted as 'peace limes' at the end of the Second World War. In some regions it was customary to plant a lime tree on the birth of the first child or as a present for a newly married couple.

The village lime tree was an important place to meet, to exchange news and to hold council. People felt able to communicate and to resolve conflicts there. The old Germanic cultures of Northern Europe held town meetings called the 'thing', where issues of public interest were presented, discussed and decided upon. In the Middle Ages, the 'thing' was the venue for court trials. It was seen as vital that the trials took place out in the open and under lime trees. People believed that lime trees supported them in their quest for truth. Opposing parties were apparently reconciled through the tree's sweet scent.

KEY SKILL: COMMUNICATION AND RESOLVING CONFLICTS

The ability to communicate and to deal with conflicts are vital social skills – in the workplace, at school, in families and relationships. This may include being able to:

Express yourself clearly
Be aware of non-verbal communication
Listen, and ask for clarification
Defend your own opinion and accept different
   opinions
Resist quick judgement or interpretation
Recognise, address and resolve conflicts
React positively to criticism

Meeting under lime trees

We can no longer be sure where the ancient places are where people communicated and solved their conflicts, yet there are still some lime trees, perhaps in a village, at the edge of a wood or in a meadow. Use the opportunity offered by the lime to enter into dialogue with others with its help and support – be it to address difficult issues within the group or to look for solutions. Conversations held underneath lime trees generally encourage a healthy social life within the group. The lime tree also helps with restlessness and lack of concentration. It has a balancing and calming effect. Regular encounters with lime trees will enhance a sense of peace and equilibrium.

Naturally, meetings held under lime trees need to be adjusted according to the age of the group. Adults, too, may wish to take advantage of such a location.

Create a circular seating arrangement. You can build a kind of 'sofa' as a group by laying down branches up to knee height and then covering them with finer material. You may wish to light a fire in the middle of the circle or build a sculpture using natural materials. A symbolic boundary around the site can be marked with sticks.

The meeting starts with a common ritual (singing, rhythmic work with stones etc.) in order to create the right mood for what's to come. Now everyone feels involved and is aware that they should be an active member of the group.

The topics may be chosen by the group, but it can be a good idea for the leader to prepare a few options beforehand. These meetings should be held as regularly as possible to develop sound habits of conversation. It's important to agree on some rules for these meetings, to keep order (see also p.86) Symbolic signs for these rules can be carved into sticks.

Within an existing long-term group (class, family) the tree meeting may become a kind of class or family conference. In a temporary group (holiday camp or holiday activity day) the lime-tree meeting mainly helps to decide on general rules, to talk about common activities and to get a clear picture about group dynamics.

Summer

HOME REMEDIES, FOOD AND COSMETICS

Lime-blossom tea is still a popular herbal remedy. The leaves, juice and bark of the lime tree also used to be collected for medicinal purposes. Charcoal made from the wood of lime trees was important in dental care and in the treatment of food poisoning (see p.127).

Lime-blossom tea increases perspiration, so is effective for treating fevers, colds and influenza. It's well known to be a relaxing, calming, even sleep-inducing remedy. It will help soothe a tickly cough and has an expectorant and antispasmodic effect. To treat conjunctivitis, apply a poultice prepared with the tea. A lime-blossom bath is also very relaxing, calming and can be a remedy for insomnia.

Pick the blossoms in early summer when they have just opened. Gather and lay them out on paper to dry in the shade. Turn them occasionally while they are drying.

Lime-blossom tea

Pour 1 litre (1 quart) of boiling water onto 4 tablespoons (for fevers 8–10 tablespoons) of lime blossoms. Infuse for 10 minutes and strain.

Lime-blossom tea is tasty and thirst-quenching at any time of year. You can also add different herbs as well. It's delicious when mixed with elderberry juice.

Sleeping tea

1 part lime blossoms
1 part lemon-balm leaves

Good-luck tea

2 parts lime blossoms
2 parts apple peel
1 part rose petals

Tea for colds

1 part lime blossoms
1 part elderflower blossoms
1 part thyme

Drink three times a day to alleviate colds and if you're feeling run-down. Sweeten to taste with lime-blossom honey.

Everyday tea

2 parts lime blossoms
1 part calendula flowers
1 part peppermint leaves

Tea for the nerves

40 g (1 1/2 oz) ground almonds
A little honey
1/2 litre (1/2 quart) lime-blossom tea

Mix the ingredients together. This tea helps to strengthen weak nerves and helps in times of stress.

Food from leaves and blossoms

Bees love lime trees. In summer, thousands are attracted by the sweet scent of the blossoms and come buzzing around the trees to collect nectar. Lime-blossom honey is delicious and healthy.

Young tender lime-tree leaves can be added to salads and soups. You can even put them into your sandwich. However, mature leaves are rather tough, but they can be made into flour. Dry the leaves, remove the veins and grind them in a coffee mill or food processor. You can add the flour to your bread and cake mixtures or to other dishes.

Lime-blossom soap

The qualities of the lime tree are also used in skincare products. Lime-blossom tea may serve as a gentle face tonic for delicate skin and it can be applied to mildly infected skin. A poultice made with lime-blossom tea soothes puffy eyes.

After washing your hair, you can rinse it with lime-blossom tea. It relaxes the scalp, which in turn makes the hair soft.

2 teaspoons almond oil
5 drops any essential oil
2 tablespoons lime-blossom tea
Yellow food colouring (optional)
10 heaped tablespoons soap flakes

Warm up the almond oil and add the essential oil. Dissolve the food colouring in the hot tea separately. Then mix all the ingredients together and knead until smooth. Form balls or cut shapes with cutters. Dry for 2 weeks.

Children prepare a fresh lime-blossom drink

Autumn

THE STORY TREE

The lime tree has often been mentioned in poems, songs and fairy tales. Many things have happened under lime trees. There are fairy tales about both wise and unfair judgements being passed under lime trees. Lime-tree stories are often about love.

Philemon and Baucis

The story of Philemon and Baucis comes from Greek mythology.

When the gods Jupiter and Mercury came down to visit Earth, the only people who received them with friendly hospitality, despite being very poor, were Philemon and Baucis, an old faithful couple. As a reward, the two old people asked not to be separated in death. Their wish was granted and they were turned into two trees embracing each other: Philemon, the man, was turned into an oak and Baucis, his wife, into a lime tree. According to this story the lime tree is a symbol for female qualities such as fertility, kindness, motherliness and everlasting life

The Frog Prince

Beside the King's castle lay a great dark forest, and under an old lime tree in the forest was a well. On very warm days, the young Princess went out into the forest and sat down by the side of the cool fountain.

When she was bored she took a golden ball, and threw it up high and caught it. This ball was her favourite toy...

You can continue this well-known fairy tale, made popular by the Brothers Grimm, in your own words and recreate it.

A story for young and old

Your own tree story

Most people can easily answer the question, 'What is your favourite tree?' They will either remember some experience in the past or talk about a tree that's dear to them now. Trees touch people in many ways. Decide on a tree that means something to you, either now or in the past, or any tree that catches your imagination. We might be touched by a tree because of its size or beauty, because of its unique shape and gestures or simply because we encounter it daily.

Tell or write down a story that connects you to your tree. Here's an example:

The Lime Tree

How I adored our lime tree. Not just because of its blossoms, which we collected every year. It was huge and appeared to me like a kind mother protecting me. I felt that when I was near it nothing would ever happen to me. Sometimes I would sit under the tree and lean against its sturdy trunk. Then I thought I could sense power streaming through me.

Once, in November, when there was a gale outside, I stood at the kitchen window and watched how the leaves were being swirled around, how they darted through the air, how the wind played with them, dropped them, picked them up again and journeyed on with them. I wanted to mingle with the leaves and join in their happy journey. With arms outstretched I tried to catch the leaves and release them back to the wind and I had to be careful not to lose my balance.

I still love lime trees. Whenever I pass a lime tree I have to stop and look up at its branches and leaves and then I remember that once, for a moment, I was allowed to be a lime-tree leaf.

(Melita)

Winter

LIME-TREE WOOD

Sculptors, wood carvers and wood turners all love to use the soft wood of the lime tree. It's very pleasant to work with because of the warmth it radiates when touched. In the Middle Ages, lime-tree wood was popular for carving altars and relief sculptures. Figures of famous saints were carved from the holy wood. Although it's not very weather proof, its soft qualities make it perfect for carving household items such as bowls, spoons and ornaments.

Worry beads

Sand a small piece of lime-tree wood (other kinds of wood are also suitable) so it fits snugly into your hand. It should feel soft and pleasing to the hand so you really enjoy carrying it with you. When you close your hand around it, you should hear its 'heart beat'. This piece of wood can help us in any situation – it connects us with the tree and allows us to share in its power.

Certain trees can help us regain our strength, others support us in achieving our goals. The energy of the 'right' wood can help us to find peace.

Making charcoal

Using a simple method, you can make quality charcoal for drawing from lime-tree twigs.

Put peeled green twigs (soft wood is most suited: lime, sycamore, hornbeam, dogwood, willow etc.) into a metal tin that closes well, after drilling a small hole in it for ventilation. Then place the tin in hot ashes – thinner twigs will need 10–20 minutes and thicker twigs will need 20–30 minutes. You can also make charcoal from other small woodland objects such as fir cones.

Charcoal made from lime-tree wood is mainly used for artwork. People also used to produce gunpowder with it. Mixed with sage powder it was used in dental care to treat gums and to freshen the breath. In addition, lime coal was a well-known remedy to help with acute poisoning, because it can bind large amounts of poison in the stomach. It's also thought to help with gastric problems.

Worry beads made from lime-tree wood

127

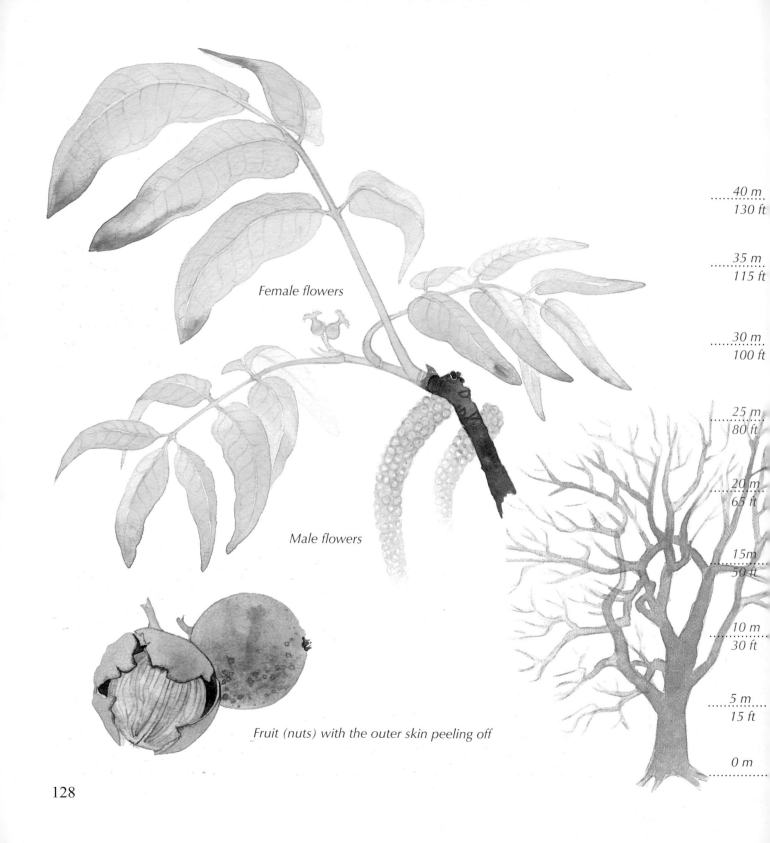

Female flowers

Male flowers

Fruit (nuts) with the outer skin peeling off

40 m
130 ft

35 m
115 ft

30 m
100 ft

25 m
80 ft

20 m
65 ft

15 m
50 ft

10 m
30 ft

5 m
15 ft

0 m

12. Walnut – Tree of Sustainability

HABITAT AND CHARACTERISTICS

Originally, the walnut tree is a native of Central Asia. It was introduced to Northern Europe by the Romans, who in turn had imported it from the Greeks. Walnut trees often grow alone in fields or near houses and along the margins of woods. They can live for about 200 years.

The tree needs a lot of space, soil rich in minerals and plenty of light. Being an immigrant from southerly regions it's very sensitive to frost. It tends to keep a distance from other trees. Plants growing in its vicinity don't thrive and grass grows only sparsely around its trunk.

The first nuts can be harvested when the tree is between three and five years old. Years with a plentiful harvest of nuts tend to alternate with poor harvests.

ALL SORTS OF USES

The walnut tree was of great importance both in mythology and as a source of food and medicine.

You can gather the leaves in late spring, the green peel in July and August, and the ripe nuts in September. In the past, the leaves of the walnut tree were made into a kind of tobacco. Because of its rich grain and beautiful colour the wood is very popular in furniture making.

Spring

SUSTAINABLE DEVELOPMENT, GIFTS AND STORIES

Sustainability is extremely important in today's world, and in the policies of economic leaders and politicians. We must avoid exhausting the Earth's natural resources, so that future generations can lead a good quality of life. The interconnectedness of all things and beings has often been explained and also misunderstood. Yet it's not difficult to explain the principles of sustainability, which become self-evident when we take examples from nature and our daily lives.

Eternal life

Once, at the time when the Prophet Mohammed was born, King Anoschirvan, whom people also called 'The Just', was wandering through his kingdom. On a sunny hill he saw an honourable old man working, with his back bent. The King, followed by his entourage, drew closer and saw that the old man was planting one-year-old shoots.

'What are you doing here?' asked the King.

'I am planting nut trees,' answered the old man.

The King wondered, 'You are already very old. Why do you still plant shoots? You won't be able to see the leaves. You won't be able to rest in its shade. You won't be able to eat the fruits.'

The old man looked up and said, 'Those who came before us planted and we were able to harvest. We plant now so that those coming after us will harvest, too.'

(From Peseschkian Nossrat, *Oriental Stories as Tools in Psychotherapy: The Merchant and the Parrot*)

The cycle of life symbolised by the nut

Sustainable gifts and wishes wrapped in a nut

You could plant a walnut. If the conditions are right, a nut tree will grow over the course of years. The tree will in turn provide us with nuts. Eventually there will be so many nuts that all of us will have enough: we can eat them, bake nut cakes, drink nut liquor etc.

At the end of its life an old nut tree may also be chopped down. Furniture can be made from the wood and when the furniture has become old and useless, it can be burnt. The wood is a source of energy for cooking a warm meal or for heating the house. The ashes can be sprinkled over the garden as fertilizer – maybe it will help a young nut tree to grow.

All these uses are possible and make sense, provided enough young trees are growing so the chain of sustainability is preserved. If we crack the last nut, then everything will have been to no avail. Today's generations have a few 'hard nuts to crack'. The problems we face today have to be solved in a sustainable way. Future generations the world over should have the opportunity not only to survive but to live life.

Sustainable gifts

As a present, you can give good wishes, symbolically 'wrapped' in nut halves. Put something you found in nature into two walnut halves, along with a good wish written down. You might want to use 'natural wrapping paper' as well. Each member of the group receives a present from someone else within the group.

Stories of sustainability

A young woman explains:'These trees give us shade in the soaring desert heat. They protect us from the sand storms which otherwise would destroy our harvest and bury our village. And they show us where to find precious drinking water.'

'Without these trees I will not be able to build a mighty castle!' says the Maharadscha.

'Without these trees we cannot survive,' says Amrita ...

(From Deborah Lee & Brigitta Säflund, *The People Who Hugged the Trees: An Environmental Folk Tale*)

Another story that fits well into this context is 'The Man Who Planted Trees' by Jean Giono (see p.49 and 'Further Reading', p.149).

Summer

HEALTH AND BEAUTY PRODUCTS

The leaves of the walnut tree and the green peel of the nuts have long since served as basic ingredients to prepare medicinal products.

Walnut-leaf tea

Briefly bring to the boil 1–2 tablespoons of chopped walnut leaves in 1 cup of water. Infuse for 10–15 minutes.

Walnut leaves are rich in tannins. They are astringent and anti-inflammatory; they are used to treat wounds, to purify the blood and to stimulate the metabolism. This tea is particularly recommended for treating skin problems, such as enlarged pores, acne, herpes, eczema, scabs and cradle cap. You can also make a poultice with the tea to relieve boils and eczema. Baths with walnut leaves alleviate skin ailments, varicose veins, rheumatism and gout.

Tea mixture

Mix equal parts of walnut leaves, pansies, stinging-nettle leaves and calendula flowers. Pour 1 cup of boiling water over 2 teaspoons of the herb mixture. Drink 2–3 cups of this tea daily to treat unclean skin.

Walnut skin oil

Put green walnut halves or walnut leaves into a glass jar and top with olive oil. Let it steep in a warm place for 3–4 weeks, strain and add essential oil of rosemary for scent.

This skin oil can be applied as a refreshing, firming massage or body oil. It used to be popular as a tanning lotion.

Nut products for new energy – tasty and effective

Nutshell syrup

Finely chop 2–3 handfuls of green nutshells. Bring to the boil in 1 litre (1 quart) of water, together with a few cloves. Infuse for 10 minutes and strain. Add 1 kg (2 1/4 lb) of raw cane sugar, boil down to syrup consistency and bottle. Take one teaspoon three times daily after meals for extra energy and as a digestive.

Natural hair care

Walnut leaves and the green nutshells have long since been used to dye wool, fabric and even hair.

Prepare a strong aqueous extract (like making tea, see p.11) from the walnut leaves or from the green shells and rinse your hair with it after washing. Brown hair will get a fresh hue and a natural shine. You can also wash your hair with tea made from walnut leaves to treat hair loss, greasy hair and dandruff.

Insect repellent

When walnut leaves are crushed they exude an intense, bitter-dry fragrance which repels insects – even bedbugs, flees, lice, mites and flies. You can hang walnut leaves in the cages of small animals, or mixed them into their straw bedding for the same purpose. Farmers liked to plant walnut trees near muck heaps to keep away flies and midges. During the Middle Ages sick rooms were disinfected by burning walnut-leaf incense.

To make insect repellent, put green nutshells or walnut leaves into a glass jar and top with olive oil. Place in the sun for 3 weeks, then strain and add a little essential oil of cloves or eucalyptus.

Special tip for happy feet

Put cooling walnut leaves into shoes to relieve burning and aching feet.

Walnut-leaf pillows

In the past, people liked to make use of the calming, sleep-inducing effect of the walnut tree. Fill a pillowcase with dried walnut leaves. When used as a pillow for sleeping, it will have a balancing, relaxing effect. Apparently it can even give your dreams a different quality.

Making a walnut-leaf pillow

Autumn

TASTY WALNUT TREATS

Autumn cheeseboard

As far back as ancient Greek and Roman times, walnuts were considered food for the gods.

Grapes, cheese and walnuts make a perfect combination for a cosy autumn evening – simply serve them together on a cheeseboard, or mix them with salad leaves and a dressing using the oil below.

Salad with walnut oil

Walnut oil is obtained by cold pressing the nuts. It's rich in linoleic acid and vitamins and has an aromatic taste, which is delicious in salad dressings. You can also mix it with neutral oil.

Put lettuce leaves, coarsely chopped walnuts and chopped onions into a bowl and mix. Trickle walnut oil and vinegar over the salad.

Pepper substitute

Poor folk used to make a pepper substitute from green walnut halves and walnut leaves. Dry green nutshells and/or walnut leaves and crush them into a powder.

FAMILY AND PLACE NAMES

Many names of villages, hamlets and families bear witness to the significance of the walnut tree and indeed of many other trees.

Who would not like to live in Five Ashes, Oaktown or Walnut Grove? Can you think of street names in your local town that have been influenced by trees? Does anybody know a family named Woods, Forrester, Ashford or Redwood? Can you find more names like that?

Walnut salad with walnut oil

Winter

KEY SKILL: CONCENTRATION AND MEMORY

Lifelong learning is a much-debated topic these days. In order to be able to learn and work successfully, effective learning strategies are needed. One of the most important factors in terms of learning is concentration – to be able to keep our attention focused on something for as long as possible. Often we can't concentrate properly because we let ourselves be distracted. Memory and concentration are dependent on the brain.

In traditional medicine walnuts were believed to strengthen the memory. As a matter of fact, the outward appearance of the nut is similar to that of the brain. Besides, the large amounts of unsaturated fatty acids in walnuts are vital for the brain's functions and the memory. Walnuts support the ability to concentrate and their high vitamin B6 content make them an ideal energy source for the entire nervous system. The walnut tree also supports us in decision-making, in times of aimlessness and mood swings. It strengthens the will and encourages clarity.

Memory oil

Chop up stinging nettles, steep in walnut oil (see p.133) and leave in a sunny place for three weeks. After straining, add some essential oil of cloves to enhance the effect. Before going to sleep, massage the oil into temples and chest. The walnut oil promotes concentration, strengthens the memory and alleviates forgetfulness and nervousness.

Walnut memory game

There are many opportunities in daily life to train the memory and encourage concentration.

To make a nut memory game, crack the nuts so the halves are as undamaged as possible. Place natural objects under the walnut halves, always two of each kind: acorns, hazelnuts, small stones and other surprises. Each player is allowed to lift up two walnut halves. If two identical objects are found, the player takes them. Whoever collects the most nutshells and their contents wins the game, and can share out any edible objects.

Tree memory game

Imagine a route that you often take, for example your way to school or work. From memory, note down all the trees you encounter on this route. Then we check if your notes are correct. Did you remember the right order and the right amount? You may want to repeat the task one more time.

Shopping-list memory game

Shopping lists are an ideal way to train the memory. Give your group one minute to memorise the following ten items on the shopping list for the 'tree shopping centre': chestnuts, rose-hip tea, walnut oil, wooden spoon, nut cake, elderberry jam, lime-blossom tea, acorn flour, wooden table, hazelnuts.

As a next step you can also memorise the following things, or any items you choose: beech nuts, spruce-needle incense, birch wood, wooden toy cow, apple cake.

How many items can everyone remember?

Order memory game

The leader blindfolds the players. One after the other, nine objects that originate from trees are placed into their hands (e.g. walnut, rose hip, leaf, piece of bark, hazelnut, chestnut, beech nut, twig, acorn). The objects are passed round in order and carefully examined by all the players so they can be recognised afterwards. It is not necessary to find the correct names for the objects (that can be another game!) but players must remember the order. The leader now arranges them in any order (after memorising the original order!) and the players have to try and lay them in the order they felt them in their hands.

Memory games are most fun when played outdoors with other children

Male flowers

Female flowers

40 m
130 ft

35 m
115 f

30 m
100 ft

25 m
80 ft

20 m
65 ft

15m
50 ft

10 m
30 ft

5 m
15 ft

0 m

138

13. Willow – Tree of Nature Spirits

HABITAT AND CHARACTERISTICS

There are countless different willow species – from small shrubs to stately trees. Willows are not very demanding in terms of their habitat; they love bright sunshine and plenty of water. By February their boughs are full of soft catkins.

The white willow is very common and it is the largest of all willow species. You can recognise them by their shiny silvery-grey leaves. Other common species in Northern Europe include weeping willow, crack willow, goat (or pussy) willow and purple willow. It's not always easy to distinguish them.

ALL SORTS OF USES

Willow rods are supple, flexible, tough and fast growing. They can be used in many ways. In times gone by, willow provided the material for various household items and people even used it for building houses. Shoes, bowls, drawing boards, matches and toothpicks were just some of the items fashioned from willow. Hollowed-out willow trunks were often made into troughs, in which dough was mixed for baking.

Poor people used to stuff their pillows with the woolly seeds of the willow. Dried willow branches and their foliage were popular animal feed in winter. Horses and sheep were even driven towards willows to feed on the quickly re-growing foliage. A decoction made from the bark was used for tanning and the leaves and roots were boiled to dye cotton fabrics. Basket makers today still use willow rods, and they are also used to build fences and small huts.

Willow trees act as windbreaks and soil improvers. They are frequently planted to prevent the erosion of riverbanks and lake shores and they are grown as pioneer plants in drainage projects. One-year-old shoots are cut from 'pollard' willows, which are commonly pruned back to the trunk at head height. Pollard willows are important natural assets: since the top section of the tree is often unsound and riddled with holes and crevices, it provides an ideal home for many different kinds of animals.

Spring

KEY SKILL: VITALITY, RENEWAL AND CONFIDENCE

In many ways the willow is a symbol of the cycle of life, of this amazing, self-renewing vitality. If you plant twigs, they will soon grow into new small trees. Pollard (cut back) willows, too, will soon sprout new shoots. The Chinese word *chi* means both 'willow' and 'breath of life'.

The wood of the willow tree is not very resilient and soon rots from the inside, so the willow also represents dying. On one hand the willow symbolises fertility, new life and renewal, and on the other hand mourning and loss.

To have self-confidence and confidence in life also requires having faith in nature's elemental powers. Death and mourning are closely connected with fertility and new life, as a sign of renewal. If we succeed in accepting these basic laws, we can feel relaxed and full of confidence in all aspects of life. The willow teaches us how to reconcile opposite poles of life; it encourages inner peace and balance.

Willow-growing experiment
The Celtic people celebrated their festival of nature's renewal in spring, at the time of the willow's flowering. They would plant willow twigs to maintain and increase the fertility of their fields. If willow twigs are planted in spring, they will soon start to sprout.

Willows love water and sun and they are incredibly fast growing. In spring, cut some rods of willow, tie them together and put them in water. After only a few days they will begin to sprout green shoots – an impressive proof of their vitality and the powers of renewal.

Willow twigs grow quickly in water

Summer

CRAFTS FROM WILLOW RODS

Green rods cut in spring may be used straight away. If the willow sticks are too dry, as is often the case in autumn, soak them in water before use. Willow rods are best cut with secateurs or pruning shears.

Making a dream catcher

Bend a willow rod to form a circle and secure with a piece of string. Weave a web into the circle using smooth string, yarn or dental floss. Work from the outside towards the centre and now and again knot natural objects, feathers or beads into the web. Leave a small hole in the centre.

Hang the dream catcher above your bed to catch your dreams. Good dreams are let through the hole to reach the sleeping person. Bad dreams are caught in the web and will disappear with the first light of day.

Willow fences

You can weave a fence or edging for your garden flowerbeds using willow rods. Put sturdy willow branches into the ground and weave thinner ones in between them. If the ground is kept moist, your fence might even sprout and come to life!

Making a fence using willow rods

Bad dreams get caught in the net of the dream catcher

Autumn

MYSTICAL WILLOW

Misty hidden valleys are believed to be the dwelling places of gnomes, fairies, magicians, tree elves and spirits of the woods and meadows. Given their often gnarled appearance and hidden spaces made by drooping branches, willows fire our imaginations. Some people have reported encountering gnomes and other mysterious beings near gnarled old willows shrouded in fog, and observing elves dance in the moonlight. So in some ways we are fascinated and also a bit wary of willows.

Making tree beings

If you wander through woods and meadows with a dreamy, unfocused look, you may be able to sense and perceive nature spirits. You can also give them a concrete form.

Use twigs and branches as a starting point to make your own magical creatures. Slightly sharpen the end of your twigs and put them in the ground for legs. Fasten on more branches and twigs with string or wire. Fir cones, chestnuts, rose hips, leaves and beech nuts can serve as eyes, ears, hair, earrings etc. Once you've finished modelling your creature you can pull it out of the ground. Tree beings like to live in balcony tubs, flowerbeds, near your front or back door, or you can create homes for them from natural objects in your garden or the woods.

You can also use a knife and a rasp to carve beings from driftwood, small branches or twigs. If you look closely, you will discover shapes in natural objects that already look like mysterious beings and spirits – nature has started to work on them already!

Witches' broomsticks

Willow trees have often been associated with witchcraft, and it's believed that witches used willow to make their flying broomsticks. Perhaps you can copy the witches and make a broom from willow branches. Who knows what magic it may contain?

Inventing tree stories

Many symbols and characteristics of the willow tree have found their way into legends, tales, songs and stories. Trees often inspire us to invent stories.

As a group, start by collecting the words you want to include in your story. For example: willow, root, sticks, searching, hungry, tree trunk, secret, shadow, sticky, old, shy, rustling, goblet.

Mysterious beings and their abodes

Children can now invent tree stories that include these words. Everyone gets a turn to choose a word and to tell a bit of the story. A magic wand made from hazel or ash helps to fire the imagination (see p.62).

Inventing your own fairy tales

Inventing a fairy tale is easier than you think. A few basic rules need to be observed. In order to succeed in creating a gripping story, the setting, the thread of the story and the characters involved have to be described in a convincing manner. Collect ideas and terms that describe your main character or central object. As a next step, add detailed information about the personality of the main characters and about the setting. Choose magic places such as caves, woods, tree houses or castles to make the story mysterious and enchanting. Involve hobgoblins, fairies, dwarves, and weave spells or magic potions into the tale. The first part of a fairy tale usually sets the scene and presents the listener with a conflict. Then there are challenges to be met along the way, and a solution needs to be found that brings redemption to the central characters. At the end of the fairy tale the conflict is resolved.

Winter

THE HEALING TREE

Beings of the earth and the air like to live in old hollow willows and their lofty branches. So it came to pass that more than a hundred years ago the fairy Loana and the gnome Sebastian lived in the same willow. Nearly every day they met to cook a meal together. Sometimes it appeared as if they could do magic, because they would feast on strawberries in the middle of winter or decorate their table with spring flowers after autumn had set in. Now and again things went wrong too. Then you had to take care when walking past the tree, because kitchen utensils would fly out from the inside of the willow, accompanied by quiet ranting and raving. Yet every time they succeeded in making up a new good recipe they would carefully write it down in their book.

Now and again human beings would come past and confide their sorrows in the willow. One winter, the people of the nearby village caught a mysterious disease. Many of them were extremely sick for weeks on end. Jacob the herbalist was on his feet day and night trying to fight the fever with tea prepared from willow bark. But since he needed such large quantities, the willow's trunk looked quite bare in many places and the willow dwellers were concerned about the health of their tree. So when Jacob turned up again, Loana and Sebastian asked him in to have a rest. They made a cup of catkin tea for Jacob and a footbath for his aching feet. When Jacob had recovered a little, he told them about his worries. More and more people in the village were falling ill. He didn't know what to do any more.

Loana and Sebastian felt they had to come up with an idea of how to make enough medicine for everyone. They studied their books and wrote down new recipes. Hissing and bubbling noises came from their tree kitchen. Sometimes small explosions were heard or sparks shot from the trunk. And lo and behold, one day they managed what they set out to make: a kind of white powder. They first tried it out themselves and then they told Jacob about their invention. The effect of the white powder was astonishing: the people's fever and headache went away and they were all well again. The invention was the talk of the whole village and soon a small shop was opened which stocked enough of the white powder to supply the people of the whole valley. The inhabitants of the village became quite famous and some of them even grew very rich.

Life in the willow became quiet again. But occasionally somebody from the village would come to the willow and confide their sorrows in it, and they would ask Loana and Sebastian for a piece of willow bark.

HOME REMEDIES

In traditional medicine, the willow was always considered to be a tree people could talk to, which would help cure their illnesses.

Nearly a hundred years ago scientists managed to produce salicin artificially, which is an active ingredient of willow bark. Acetylsalicylic acid has since been on the market all over the world in form of aspirin tablets and it is sold as chemical pain relief. Nowadays natural willow preparations are having a renaissance. They have a longer lasting and gentler action. Willow catkins are recommended to treat weak nerves, sleeplessness, menstrual problems and agitation. High doses of willow preparations, especially during pregnancy, are to be avoided.

Willow-bark tea and tincture

Tea or tincture made from willow bark is used to alleviate fevers, colds, headaches, sciatic pain, nerve pain, rheumatism, gout and arthritis. It can also be taken as a gargle to help with swollen glands. Scrape off the bark of roughly three-year-old branches and chop it up. You can also dry the bark to store it. Soak 1 teaspoon of chopped bark in a cup of water overnight, then briefly bring it to the boil. Drink 2 cups of this tea daily.

Footbath

People who have to stand or walk a lot will appreciate a refreshing footbath made with willow leaves. Mix equal parts willow leaves and mugwort, boil them in water and strain.

A footbath will also refresh tired, sweaty feet. Boil a handful of willow leaves or bark in water.

References

Cornell, Joseph, *Sharing Nature with Children: The Classic Parents' and Teachers' Nature Awareness Guidebook*, Dawn Publications, Nevada City.

De Pulford, Nicola, *Spells and Charms*, Godsfield Press, London.

Fischer-Rizzi, Susanne, *The Complete Incense Book*, Sterling Publishing, New York.

Giono, Jean, *The Man Who Planted Trees*, Harvill Press, London.

Lee, Deborah & Brigitta Säflund, *The People Who Hugged the Trees: An Environmental Folk Tale*, Roberts Rinehart Publishers.

Nossrat, Peseschkian, *Oriental Stories As Tools in Psychotherapy: The Merchant and the Parrot*, Springer.

Further Reading

Adolphi, Sybille, *Making Fairy Tale Scenes*, Floris Books, Edinburgh.

—, *Making Flower Children*, Floris Books, Edinburgh

—, *Making More Flower Children*, Floris Books, Edinburgh.

Andersen, Hans Christian, *Favourite Tales from Hans Christian Andersen*, Floris Books, Edinburgh.

Anschütz, Marieke, *Children and their Temperaments*, Floris Books, Edinburgh.

Barz, Brigitte, *Festivals with Children*, Floris Books, Edinburgh.

Bauer, John, *Swedish Folk Tales*, Floris Books, Edinburgh.

Berger, Petra, *Feltcraft*, Floris Books, Edinburgh.

Berger, Thomas, *The Christmas Craft Book*, Floris Books, Edinburgh.

Berger, Thomas & Petra, *Crafts through the Year*, Floris Books, Edinburgh.

—, *The Gnome Craft Book*, Floris Books, Edinburgh.

Clouder, Chris & Martyn Rawson, *Waldorf Education*, Floris Books, Edinburgh.

Colum, Padraic, *Myths of the World*, Floris Books, Edinburgh.

Crossley, Diana, *Muddles, Puddles and Sunshine*, Hawthorn Press, Stroud.

Dancy, Rahima Baldwin, *You are your Child's First Teacher*, Hawthorn Press, Stroud.

Drescher, Daniela, *Over the Hills and Far Away: Stories of Dwarfs, Fairies, Gnomes and Elves From Around Europe*, Floris Books, Edinburgh.

Evans, Russell, *Helping Children to Overcome Fear*, Hawthorn Press, Stroud.

Grimm, Jacob & Wilhelm, *Favourite Grimm's Tales*, Floris Books, Edinburgh.

Guéret, Frédérique, *Magical Window Stars*, Floris Books, Edinburgh.

Jaffke, Freya, *Work and Play in Early Childhood*, Floris Books, Edinburgh & Anthroposophic Press, New York.

—, *Celebrating Festivals with Children*, Floris Books, Edinburgh.

— & Dagmar Schmidt, Magic Wool: *Creative Pictures and Tableaux with Natural Sheep's Wool*, Floris Books, Edinburgh.

Jenkinson, Sally, *The Genius of Play*, Hawthorn Press, Stroud.

König, Karl, *The First Three Years of the Child*, Floris Books, Edinburgh.

Kornberger, Horst, *The Power of Stories*, Floris Books, Edinburgh.

Kutsch, Irmgard and Brigitte Walden, *Spring Nature Activities for Children,* Floris Books, Edinburgh.

—, *Summer Nature Activities for Children,* Floris Books, Edinburgh.

—, *Autumn Nature Activities for Children,* Floris Books, Edinburgh.

—, *Winter Nature Activities for Chidren,* Floris Books, Edinburgh.

Kraul, Walter, *Earth, Water, Fire and Air,* Floris Books, Edinburgh.

de La Fontaine, Jean, *The Fables of La Fontaine,* Floris Books, Edinburgh.

Leeuwen, M van & J Moeskops, *The Nature Corner,* Floris Books, Edinburgh.

Mellon, Nancy, *Storytelling with Children,* Hawthorn Press, Stroud.

Meyer, Rudolf, *The Wisdom of Fairy Tales,* Floris Books, Edinburgh.

Müller, Brunhild, *Painting with Children,* Floris Books, Edinburgh.

Murray, Lorraine E., *Calm Kids: Help Children Relax with Mindful Activities,* Floris Books, Edinburgh.

Neuschütz, Karin, *Sewing Dolls,* Floris Books, Edinburgh.

—, *Creative Wool,* Floris Books, Edinburgh.

Oldfield, Lynne, *Free to Learn,* Hawthorn Press, Stroud.

Petrash, Carol, *Earthwise: Environmental Crafts and Activities with Young Children,* Floris Books, Edinburgh & Gryphon House, Maryland.

Rawson, Martyn & Michael Rose, *Ready to Learn,* Hawthorn Press, Stroud.

Reinhard, Rotraud, *A Felt Farm,* Floris Books, Edinburgh.

Reinckens, Sunnhild, *Making Dolls,* Floris Books, Edinburgh.

Santer, Ivor, *Green Fingers and Muddy Boots,* Floris Books, Edinburgh.

Schäfer, Christine, *Magic Wool Fairies,* Floris Books, Edinburgh.

Sealey, Maricristin, *Kinder Dolls,* Hawthorn Press, Stroud.

Steiner, Rudolf, *The Education of the Child in the Light of Anthroposophy,* Steiner Press, London, & Anthroposophic Press, New York.

Taylor, Michael, *Finger Strings,* Floris Books, Edinburgh.

Thomas, Anne & Peter, *The Children's Party Book,* Floris Books, Edinburgh

Thomas, Heather, *A Journey Through Time in Verse and Rhyme,* Floris Books, Edinburgh.

Wolck-Gerche, Angelika, *Creative Felt,* Floris Books, Edinburgh.

—, *More Magic Wool,* Floris Books, Edinburgh.

—, *Papercraft,* Floris Books, Edinburgh.

SPRING
nature activities for children

Irmgard Kutsch & Brigitte Walden

Irmgard Kutsch & Brigitte Walden
ISBN 978–086315–544–4

SUMMER
nature activities for children

Irmgard Kutsch & Brigitte Walden

Irmgard Kutsch & Brigitte Walden
ISBN 978–086315–586–4

AUTUMN
nature activities for children

Irmgard Kutsch & Brigitte Walden

Irmgard Kutsch & Brigitte Walden
ISBN 978–086315–495–9

WINTER
nature activities for children

Irmgard Kutsch & Brigitte Walden

Irmgard Kutsch & Brigitte Walden
ISBN 978–086315–564–2

www.florisbooks.co.uk

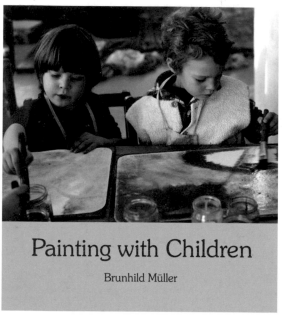

Painting with Children
Brunhild Müller

Brunhild Müller
ISBN 978–086315–366–2

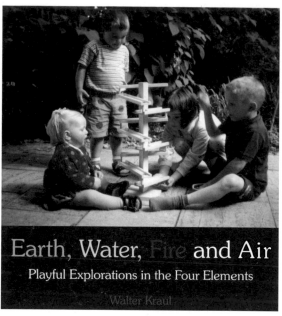

Earth, Water, Fire and Air
Playful Explorations in the Four Elements
Walter Kraul

Walter Kraul
ISBN 978–086315–768–4

Earthwise
Environmental Crafts and
Activities with Young Children

CAROL PETRASH

Carol Petrash
ISBN 978–086315–158–3

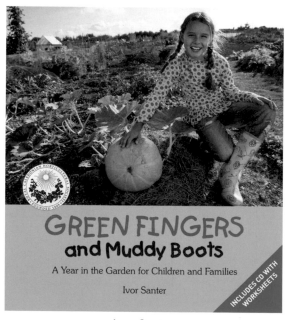

GREEN FINGERS
and Muddy Boots
A Year in the Garden for Children and Families
Ivor Santer

INCLUDES CD WITH WORKSHEETS

Ivor Santer
ISBN 978–086315–692–2

www.florisbooks.co.uk